BAPTISTWAY®

Adult Bible Study Guide

The Gospel of John

So That You May Believe

Charles Bugg
Kathy Robinson Hillman
David Morgan

BAPTISTWAY PRESS®
Dallas, Texas

BAPTISTWAY PRESS® Management Team
Executive Director, Baptist General Convention of Texas: Charles Wade
Coordinator, Church Health and Growth Section: H. Lynn Eckeberger
Director, Bible Study/Discipleship Center: Dennis Parrott
Administrator, Curriculum Development: Bernard M. Spooner

Publishing consultant: Ross West, Positive Difference Communications
Cover and Interior Design and Production: Desktop Miracles, Inc.
Front Cover Photo: Scene from Galilee, BiblePlaces.com

First edition: March 2003
ISBN: 1–931060–32–0

How to Make the Best Use of This Issue

Whether you're the teacher or a student—

1. Start early in the week before your class meets.
2. Overview the study. Look at the table of contents, read the study introduction, and read the unit introduction for the lesson you're about to study. Try to see how each lesson relates to the unit and overall study of which it is a part.
3. Use your Bible to read and consider prayerfully the Scripture passages for the lesson. (You'll see that each writer has chosen a favorite translation for each unit in this issue. You're free to use the Bible translation you prefer and compare it with the translation chosen for that unit, of course.)
4. After reading all the Scripture passages in your Bible, then read the writer's comments. The comments are intended to be an aid to your study of the Bible.
5. Read the small articles—"sidebars"—in each lesson. They are intended to provide additional, enrichment information and inspiration and to encourage thought and application.
6. Try to answer for yourself the questions included in each lesson. They're intended to encourage further thought and application, and they can also be used in the class session itself.

If you're the teacher—

A. Do all of the things just mentioned, of course.
B. In the first session of the study, briefly overview the study by identifying with your class the date on which each lesson will be studied. Lead your class to write the date in the table of contents on page 5 and on the first page of each lesson. You might also find it helpful to make and post a chart that indicates the date on which each lesson will be studied. If all of your class has e-mail, send them an e-mail with the dates the lessons will be studied.
C. You may want to get the enrichment teaching help that is provided in the *Baptist Standard* and/or on the internet. Call 214–630–4571 to begin your subscription to the *Baptist Standard*. Access the internet information by checking the *Baptist Standard* website at

http://www.baptiststandard.com. (Other class participants may find this information helpful, too.)

D. Get a copy of the *Teaching Guide*, which is a companion piece to these lesson comments. It contains additional Bible comments plus two teaching plans. The teaching plans in the *Teaching Guide* are intended to provide practical, easy-to-use teaching suggestions that will work in your class.

E. After you've studied the Bible passage, the lesson comments, and other material, use the teaching suggestions in the *Teaching Guide* to help you develop your plan for leading your class in studying each lesson.

F. Enjoy leading your class in discovering the meaning of the Scripture passages and in applying these passages to their lives.

John: So That You May Believe

UNIT FOUR

Jesus' Glorious Triumph

JOHN: *So That You May Believe*

The Gospel of John is at once simple and profound. It is so simple that this gospel has often been used to introduce people to Jesus and lead them to place their faith in him. As the purpose of the Gospel of John states: "Now Jesus did many other signs in the presence of his disciples, which are not written in this book. But these are written so that you may come to believe that Jesus is the Messiah, the Son of God, and that through believing you may have life in his name" (John 20:31, NRSV[1]).

In the midst of this apparent simplicity, however, there is also great depth, even mystery. We see this from the very first verse: "In the beginning was the Word, and the Word was with God, and the Word was God" (1:1). For all their simplicity, those words contain deep meaning. Moreover, as this gospel moves through its treatment of Jesus, what he did, and how people responded to him, it interacts with Greek and Jewish religious traditions of many kinds. Underneath what seems so simple on the surface can be found references to how the Christian faith related to various complex clusters of first-century ideas. These interactions are sometimes not apparent from mere surface reading or study.

Simple and easy to understand; profound and mysterious—that is the Gospel of John. But how could we expect otherwise? After all, the subject of the Gospel of John is God becoming flesh in a human being. Not only that, it is the account of this human being, Jesus, in whom God was uniquely present, giving his life and being rejected by "his own people" (1:11). What kind of God is this? How could this happen? The Gospel of John calls us to ponder such questions rather than merely to consider interesting stories and sayings.

A brilliant Baptist interpreter of the Gospel of John, George Beasley-Murray,[2] now gone to be with the Lord of whom this gospel is written, said that new believers can find in John a wonderful exposition of the faith they have embraced. Also, mature Christians can continue to find their faith illumined as they learn more of Jesus through this gospel. Too, the aged Christian can learn even more of the glory of God as it is revealed in this gospel. Further, those who are dying can find comfort in its words that tell of Jesus, who brings peace, comfort, and hope. Let us add that those who have not yet believed can be led to believe through a study of this gospel.

Which vantage point in the preceding paragraph is yours? Whatever the case, as you study this gospel, let John's message speak to you. Consider several ways of approaching this study that will help you do just that.

First, plan to study John with keen attention and a willingness to learn what John's Gospel has to teach. Avoid assuming that you have "heard this story before" and thus know all about it. Studying John with the attitude that you are crossing territory so familiar you can do it with your eyes closed is a sure way not to learn much of anything on this particular journey.

Second, consider the meaning behind the familiar stories and sayings. As is often the case with the Bible, many readers of the Gospel of John have focused on the stories and the sayings—Jesus turning the water into wine (John 2); Jesus talking with Nicodemus (John 3); Jesus talking with the Samaritan woman (John 4); Jesus healing the paralyzed man (John 5); plus John 3:16. However, they have neither sought nor found the interconnectedness and the powerful insights that carry John's message along and reveal who Jesus is. In particular, Jesus' extended teachings in John 6—12 are often passed by in favor of the stories of Jesus' feeding the multitude (John 6) and healing the blind man (John 9). These teachings, however, provide needed explanation of the significance of these events. Resolve not merely to see the interesting stories but also to seek their meaning.

Third, let the Gospel of John speaks its own unique message about Jesus. Don't run too quickly to the other gospels, particularly to try to harmonize the flow of events. Seek to understand John's Gospel on its own terms. Each of the gospels has its own unique approach to Jesus and his significance. Each gospel tells and interprets Jesus' story in a special way for its own focused purpose.

There has long been general agreement that Matthew, Mark, and Luke have great similarities, that Mark was the first written gospel, and that Matthew and Luke show dependence on Mark. John, however, stands to itself to an even greater extent than do the other three gospels.

Have you ever heard or sung a familiar hymn text set to a different tune? Often when this is done, the hymn text takes on new meaning and causes us to worship in new and unexpected ways. We might say that each of the gospel writers set the text of Jesus' life, ministry, death, and resurrection to a different tune. Moreover, each of them used somewhat different words, with John's words being quite different. Each gospel's "hymn" still calls us to know and serve the risen Christ, however.

Think of what we would miss if we did not have this gospel. Were it not for the Gospel of John, we would not know of Jesus' extensive ministry in Jerusalem earlier than the week of his death. Indeed, we would not even know of the likelihood of a three-year ministry of Jesus. The timeline of the other gospels can be put into a single year, while John alone mentions three passovers (see 2:13; 6:4; 11:55). Even more important, we would not see as clearly the linkage between Jesus' death and his ministry if we did not have John's Gospel.

So, for this study, pay attention to John's Gospel and what it tells about Jesus and his significance for your life. Let this study lead you to the abundant life of which John speaks, which Jesus offers to those who will believe in him. Jesus' words still ring true for us: "I came that they may have life, and have it abundantly" (10:10).

The last verse of the Gospel of John states: "But there are also many other things that Jesus did; if every one of them were written down, I suppose that the world itself could not contain the books that would be written" (21:25). We might also apply the spirit of that verse to Bible study lessons. The Bible study lesson possibilities in the Gospel of John are many. Out of many possibilities, thirteen Bible study lessons have been projected for this study. The thirteen lessons are divided into four units. These units and the lessons within them attempt to follow the contours of the Gospel of John itself and to encourage us to get at the heart of its message as we study.

Unit One, "The Word and His Works," consists of five lessons from John 1—5. The unit begins with a study of what is known as the prologue (1:1–18). The prologue introduces the entire book and points to its meaning. The next four lessons are on the following incidents: Jesus' first sign, at the wedding at Cana (John 2); Jesus' conversation with Nicodemus (John 3); Jesus' conversation with the Samaritan woman (John 4); and Jesus' healing of the lame man (John 5).

Unit Two, "The Growing Conflict," is a two-lesson study of John 6—10. The first lesson in this unit is from John 6 and focuses on Jesus' interpretation of the meaning of the feeding of the multitude. The second lesson in the unit considers Jesus' healing of the blind man and the meaning of that event, according to John 9—10. These lessons show the growing conflict between Jesus and the Jewish leaders.

Additional Resources for Studying the Gospel of John:[3]

George R. Beasley-Murray. *John*. Word Biblical Commentary. Volume 36. Waco, Texas: Word Books, Publisher, 1987.

Raymond E. Brown. *The Gospel According to John (I—XII)*. Garden City, New York: Doubleday & Company, Inc., 1966.

Raymond E. Brown. *The Gospel According to John (XIII—XXI)*. Garden City, New York: Doubleday & Company, Inc., 1970.

F.F. Bruce. *The Gospel of John*. Grand Rapids, Michigan: William B. Eerdmans Publishing Company, 1983.

James E. Carter. *John*. Layman's Bible Book Commentary. Volume 18. Nashville: Broadman Press, 1984.

Herschel H. Hobbs. *The Gospel of John: Invitation to Life*. Nashville, Tennessee: Convention Press, 1988.

William E. Hull. "John." *The Broadman Bible Commentary*. Volume 9. Nashville, Tennessee: Broadman Press, 1970.

Leon Morris. *The Gospel According to John*. The New International Commentary on the New Testament. Grand Rapids: Wm. B. Eerdmans, 1971.

Lesslie Newbigin. *The Light Has Come: An Exposition of the Fourth Gospel*. Grand Rapids, Michigan: William B. Eerdmans Publishing Company, 1982.

Gail R. O'Day. "The Gospel of John." *The New Interpreter's Bible*. Volume IX. Nashville, Tennessee: Abingdon Press, 1995.

Unit Three, "The Time Has Come," provides a two-lesson study of John 11—12. With Jesus' raising of Lazarus from death, the opposition of the Pharisees came to a head with the decision to kill Jesus. The first lesson of the unit is a study of the raising of Lazarus in John 11. (This lesson is for study on Easter in the first year of release of these materials.) The second lesson focuses on Jesus' offer of himself as the Savior of the world in John 11:55—12:50. In this unit, we will see that both the Jewish leaders and Jesus considered that "the time had come." At this point, the Jewish leaders began to seek to kill Jesus (11:53), and Jesus stated that his "hour" had come (12:23).

Unit Four, "Jesus' Glorious Triumph," relates to Jesus' death and resurrection and consists of four lessons on John 13—21. The first treats Jesus' example of service in John 13, and the second considers portions of Jesus' farewell discourse in John 14—17. The emphasis in both of these lessons is on Jesus' preparation of the disciples for life after his death. The third lesson of this unit is a study of John's portrayal of Jesus' death on the cross in John 19. The final lesson of the study is on Jesus' resurrection appearances to Mary, the disciples, and Thomas (John 20).

NOTES

1. Unless otherwise indicated, all Scripture quotations in this article are from the New Revised Standard Version Bible, copyright 1989, Division of Christian Education of the National Council of the Churches of Christ in the United States of America. Used by permission. All rights reserved.
2. George R. Beasley-Murray, *John*, Word Biblical Commentary, vol. 36 (Waco, Texas: Word Books, Publisher, 1987), x.
3. Listing a book does not imply full agreement by the writers or BAPTISTWAY PRESS® with all of its comments.

The Word and His Works

Unit One, The Word and His Works, consists of five lessons on John 1—5. The unit begins with a study of what is known as the prologue (John 1:1–18). The prologue introduces the entire gospel and points to its meaning. The next four lessons are as follows: Jesus' first sign, at the wedding at Cana (John 2); Jesus' conversation with Nicodemus (John 3); Jesus' conversation with the Samaritan woman (John 4); and Jesus' healing of the lame man (John 5).

The Scriptures to be studied in these lessons emphasize Jesus' identity. Who is he? In answering that question, these Scriptures call for belief in Jesus as the Messiah, in accord with the stated purpose of John's Gospel (see John 20:31).[1] As you study these lessons, consider afresh or for the first time the significance of Jesus for your life—particularly at this stage of your life, whatever that may be.

UNIT ONE, THE WORD AND HIS WORKS

Lesson 1	God in the Flesh	John 1:1–18
Lesson 2	Whatever Jesus Tells You	John 2:1–22
Lesson 3	For God So Loved	John 3:1–16
Lesson 4	If You Knew the Gift of God	John 4:4–30, 39–42
Lesson 5	The Case for Jesus	John 5:1–24, 31–40

NOTES

1. Unless otherwise indicated, all Scripture quotations in Unit One are from the New Revised Standard Version Bible, copyright 1989, Division of Christian Education of the National Council of the Churches of Christ in the United States of America. Used by permission. All rights reserved.

Focal Text

John 1:1–18

Background

John 1

Main Idea

In Jesus the eternal Word became flesh, revealing God uniquely and offering those who trust in him the right to become God's children.

Question to Explore

Who is Jesus, really?

Study Aim

To explain the significance for my life of who Jesus is

Study and Action Emphases

- Affirm the Bible as our authoritative guide for life and ministry
- Share the gospel with all people
- Develop a growing, vibrant faith

LESSON ONE

God in the Flesh

Quick Read

In the life and ministry of Jesus, the eternal God revealed himself to people—to you and me—in a unique manner. Indeed, in Jesus, God "became flesh and lived among us" (John 1:11). Because God came in this manner, we can know more of what God is like. Even more important, we can enter more fully and more personally into relationship with God.

I have always loved Christmas pageants. Children in soccer uniforms and dance outfits race into the church house, and they are suddenly transformed into angels, shepherds, wise men, Mary, and Joseph.

The Gospel of John has no nativity narrative, however. In the Gospel of John, Jesus emerges full-blown on the human scene as God. The Gospel of John wants us to understand that Jesus is divine as well as human.

We still ask, *Who is Jesus?* This gospel provides a powerful response.

Who Is Jesus? (1:1–5)

This question is the fundamental question of the Christian faith. Books have been written about who Jesus is. In fact, recently a number of books have been published speculating about the nature and mission of Jesus. Was Jesus a peasant preacher, a political revolutionary, an itinerant healer? Or was Jesus first and foremost the Son of God?

The nature of Jesus is not just the subject of books. The most important question is, *Who is Jesus for you and me?* You and I may write a book about the subject of marriage, but that doesn't make us married. To be married is to commit ourselves to a person with whom we agree to share life.

The intent of the Gospel of John is to call each of us to enter into a personal relationship with Jesus (see John 20:30–31). John wants us first, however, to understand this divine/human person whom we promise to love. To explain who Jesus is, John used the Greek word *logos*. In most of our English translations, *logos* is translated "the Word."

What is this *logos* of God? This Greek term would have been familiar to John's first-century readers. Remember, the news of Jesus was moving into all of the world of that day. Many who heard it had been heavily influenced by Greek thought. John was doing what a good teacher does. With the inspiration of the Holy Spirit, John was communicating with ideas and images that his audience would have understood.

While *logos* has multiple shades of meaning, "Word" is a good translation for us. The Gospel of John talks about the nature of God's clearest communication to humankind. Jesus is that "Word." Just as the words we speak communicate a message, the gospel writer wants us to see Jesus as the ultimate word or message from God.

John wants us to know some important facts about Jesus, whom John calls "the Word." First, John wants you and me to understand clearly that

John 1:1–18

¹In the beginning was the Word, and the Word was with God, and the Word was God. ²He was in the beginning with God. ³All things came into being through him, and without him not one thing came into being. What has come into being ⁴in him was life, and the life was the light of all people. ⁵The light shines in the darkness, and the darkness did not overcome it.

⁶There was a man sent from God, whose name was John. ⁷He came as a witness to testify to the light, so that all might believe through him. ⁸He himself was not the light, but he came to testify to the light. ⁹The true light, which enlightens everyone, was coming into the world.

¹⁰He was in the world, and the world came into being through him; yet the world did not know him. ¹¹He came to what was his own, and his own people did not accept him. ¹²But to all who received him, who believed in his name, he gave power to become children of God, ¹³who were born, not of blood or of the will of the flesh or of the will of man, but of God.

¹⁴And the Word became flesh and lived among us, and we have seen his glory, the glory as of a father's only son, full of grace and truth. ¹⁵(John testified to him and cried out, "This was he of whom I said, 'He who comes after me ranks ahead of me because he was before me.'") ¹⁶From his fullness we have all received, grace upon grace. ¹⁷The law indeed was given through Moses; grace and truth came through Jesus Christ. ¹⁸No one has ever seen God. It is God the only Son, who is close to the Father's heart, who has made him known.

Jesus is completely divine. The initial verse of John's Gospel sets the tone for everything that follows: "In the beginning was the Word, and the Word was with God, and the Word was God."

If that is hard for us to understand, we are in good company. One of the most difficult questions with which Christians have wrestled has been the nature of God. In seeking to understand God's nature, we Christians refer to God as the Trinity. As believers, we are careful to say that God is one and that this God is manifested in three ways—the Father, the Son, and the Holy Spirit.

In talking about Jesus, the Gospel of John does not explain how the Son could both *be with* God and *be* God. These ideas in the very first verse of John's Gospel remind us that there are parts of our faith beyond human understanding. For example, I can't physically *be with* somebody and *be* that somebody. However, if I attempt to explain all of the Bible in ways that I can understand, I will wind up with a very small Bible.

The Gospel of John wants to make very clear that Jesus is divine and, therefore, that God works in ways beyond all human comprehension. How sad it would be to believe in a God whose ways were always our ways and whose thoughts were only the projection of our thoughts.

The Bible presents a God who is beyond human capacity to explain fully. God comes to us, dwells with us, and redeems us, but, as Paul said, "We see through a glass, darkly" (1 Corinthians 13:12, KJV). We never fully understand God because God is God, and we are human beings.

Recently my daughter was married. My wife and I were excited. We have come to love the young man whom Laura Beth married. At the rehearsal the day before the wedding, I was leading the rehearsal since I was to perform the wedding. I said, "We'll begin the ceremony with my saying a few words about the meaning of marriage." Suddenly, Laura Beth started crying, my wife was dabbing her eyes, and I had some tears trickling down my cheeks.

We still ask, Who is Jesus?

What was happening? Why were we crying at the rehearsal? In part the reason was that as a family we understood that profound changes had taken place. My daughter had become a young woman. When she was a little girl, Laura Beth's needs were fairly simple. If she scraped her knee,

Logos

Translated "Word" in the Gospel of John (1:1), *logos* has a rich tradition in the Old Testament and in Greek philosophical thought. While *logos* is difficult to define, it may refer to a word, a sentence, or an argument designed to communicate. In Greek Stoic philosophy, *logos* is used to designate the divine order that guides and directs the universe.

In Jewish Scriptures, the "word" from God spoke the world into being (Genesis 1). Thus, the "word" can create or recreate. In the wisdom literature of the Old Testament, such as the Book of Proverbs, this creative power of God is personified (see Proverbs 8:22–36).

The Gospel of John uses these various strains of thought in describing the "Word" in 1:1–18. What emerges is a person named Jesus, who is both divine and human. Jesus, "the Word," communicates the truth about who God is and how we can know God in our lives.

she could run to her mommy or to me. We would kiss it, and that would help to make it well.

Now that she's a young woman, she's much more complex. She's grown in her capacity to love. Laura Beth is now able to say to Brian, "I love you, and I want to share my life with you." Diane's and my relationship to our child is different. She's an adult. While she's still our daughter, Laura Beth has grown up. She makes decisions, fixes her own scrapes, and in a wonderful way has become more of a mystery to her parents. We can't explain what she does and why she does it as easily as we once could.

That's the way a mature relationship should be. We love the person, but we don't need to control. We allow for the mysterious. We accept what we can't always understand.

Why not do the same with God? We love God, but we don't always understand. We put our faith in Jesus as the Son of God, which really means that we trust Jesus to be in control.

When the Gospel of John talks about the future ministry of Jesus, it uses two key words, "life" and "light." The Gospel says, "What has come into being in him was life, and the life was the light of all people. The light shines in the darkness, and the darkness did not overcome it" (John 1:3b–5).

> *The most important question is, Who is Jesus for you and me?*

John's Gospel wants us to understand several important changes Jesus makes in us. First, Jesus brings us life. John is speaking about what we often refer to as "eternal life." Eternal life means not only that we have life with God after our physical death but also that we can live in this world with a new power and a new peace.

Recently I went to a large metropolitan area that has a huge medical center. Down the street from the medical center was the church where I preached. I couldn't help but be struck by the contrast. The medical center with all of its vast resources is seeking to extend the quantity of people's lives. There's nothing wrong with that. We applaud the advances in medical care.

In the shadow of the medical complex sat the church. The church, too, has a message about life. However, that message is about the quality of life. The church proclaims that through trust in Jesus Christ, you and I can live in the present with peace and purpose. To follow Christ is to live forever with God. That life begins in the now.

John said that Jesus, the life, brings light (1:4). John's Gospel speaks often about the contest between light and darkness (see 1:5, 7–9; 3:19–21; 8:12; 9:5; 11:9–10; 12:35–36, 46).

The Gospel of John never says that a follower of Jesus is made immune from the valleys and shadows of this life. When our son was ten years old, he was diagnosed with a brain tumor. I watched David endure radiation treatments and life-threatening surgeries. David has survived, and for that I'm enormously grateful. But he's limited in what he can do, and I will always remember his pain and suffering.

> *The Gospel of John is clear . . . that neither the darkness of suffering nor the darkness of sin can overcome or defeat the light of Christ.*

Why do these things happen? I don't know. As a pastor and preacher, I have wanted to give myself and others a good answer. About all I can say is that we live in a world where darkness is pervasive, and that suffering thus comes to the just and the unjust.

The Gospel of John is clear, however, that neither the darkness of suffering nor the darkness of sin can overcome or defeat the light of Christ. This is authentic Christian hope. The Gospel of John tells us about people who do dark things, the darkest of which is to kill Jesus. Sin abounds. Suffering abounds. On the third day, Jesus emerged alive from the tomb. Here's the good news. The light shines in the darkness. The darkness doesn't understand it, and the darkness doesn't conquer it (1:5). The light of God shines.

Who Is John? (1:6–9)

Before Jesus came a man named John. Who was John? This John is different from the one referred to as the writer of the Gospel of John. Some people called this John, "the baptizer" (see Mark 1:4). That is how this John is described in Matthew, Mark, and Luke. John immersed people in rivers as a sign that they had turned to God. The Gospel of John identifies this forerunner of Jesus as a "witness . . . to the light" (1:7). John the baptizer was not the revelation of God. The job of John the baptizer was to witness—to tell the truth, the whole truth, and nothing but the truth about Jesus, the ultimate

> *When we receive Jesus into our lives, we can live with new purpose, new power, and new peace.*

God and the Letters of Our Lives

A little girl was saying her bedtime prayers. Her bedroom door was ajar. Her father passed by and listened. When the girl had finished, she looked up to see her dad.

"I couldn't help but hear what you were praying. You were saying the alphabet," her dad said.

"Daddy," the girl replied, "I couldn't think of what to say to God tonight. So I said, 'God, here are the letters of my life. You put them together however you want.'"

When we believe Jesus is really God, we give Jesus who we are and let him put us together the way he wants.

---

revelation of God. John cried out that God had come in Jesus. This truth is the most profound we can ever know. God wants to be known. The job of John the baptizer was to announce that and to call everyone to realize this truth.

Evidently John was an impressive figure. He ate strange foods; he wore unusual clothes; his sanctuary was the desert (Mark 1:6). However, his message was straightforward. He boldly called people to repent—to turn back to God (Mark 1:4). He wasn't afraid to preach it as he saw it. What happened was that some people became so enamored of John the witness that they began to follow him.

Before we become too critical of those who gave their primary allegiance to John instead of Jesus, maybe we had better ask

In his crucifixion, Jesus showed how much God loves us, but the fact is that many people don't know and don't care.

ourselves if that ever happens to us. Have you ever had a pastor whom you held in such high esteem that you felt no one could ever replace such a person? Have you ever had a teacher you loved so much you refused to be promoted on "Promotion Day" in Sunday School? You were surrounded in your class by people thirty years younger, but you couldn't bear the thought of going to another class! Only Mrs. Murphy could teach the Bible the way it should be taught.

Sometimes this loyalty to a person can create severe problems. I know a church where the pastor was almost everything anybody could want in a minister. One day he revealed a moral lapse. Some members were so devastated that they stopped attending church. The minister was also devastated by what he had done. After months of therapy, his relationship with his wife was restored. He continued, though, to carry great regret for the disappointment that people had in him. This pastor had never wanted to be put on a pedestal. He had never wanted the worship of others. He wanted to be a witness. Unfortunately, some church members saw him as "the light."

What Does the Word's Becoming Flesh Mean? (1:10–18)

These verses describe and explain "the true light" which "was coming into the world" (1:9). They portray the One of whom John the baptizer testified. In 1:10–18, we see again that the Gospel of John is concerned that its readers understand theologically who Jesus is.

According to the Gospel of John, the greatest truth we can ever know is not truth about something but truth about Someone.

In these verses, the Gospel of John sets forth the significance of Jesus. The Gospel of John also wants us to understand that not everybody welcomed Jesus as the gift of God. Indeed, the people among whom Jesus was born and lived in Israel did not receive him. While Jesus is the "glory" of God (1:14), people don't always recognize that glory. In fact, John later used the idea to refer to Jesus' death (see John 13:31–32). In his crucifixion, Jesus showed how much God loves us, but the fact is that many people don't know and don't care.

Wonderfully, however, some did and do receive Jesus by believing in him (1:12). This passage indicates the opportunity of choice that God makes available to us. To those who thus receive him, Jesus gives "power to become children of God" (1:12). They enter the richness of an intimate relationship with God as Father and themselves as God's children.

How sad it would be to believe in a God whose ways were always our ways and whose thoughts were only the projection of our thoughts.

Verse 13 affirms that such a relationship is not possible by human means. Birth to such a new life occurs only through the power of God (look ahead to 3:3, 8).

Perhaps you have read John 1:14 so many times that when you read it you miss how shocking it must have been to many who read it then and still is to many who read it now. What a message! "The Word became flesh and lived among us" (1:14). To people who saw God as distant and even unapproachable, this statement is a theological lightning bolt. It shows the uniqueness of who Jesus is. It shows also how far God in love has come to reach even to us (see 3:16).

Verse 15 reminds us again that this Jesus, the Word in whom we see God's "glory," was the One of whom John the baptizer was testifying. Verses 19–42 tell of specific instances in which John the baptizer pointed to Jesus. John denied he was the Christ but explained his role only as one who pointed to Jesus as the Christ (1:19–28). He called Jesus "the Son of God" at Jesus' baptism (1:29–34). He even advised directly two of his disciples that Jesus was the One to whom he was pointing (1:25–42; see 3:25–30; 5:31–36 for more on John's role).

To follow Christ is to live forever with God.

In verses 16–18, the Gospel of John contrasts the law of Moses and the grace and truth that came through Jesus. These verses also suggest that although Moses knew God in a close manner (see Exodus 33:20–23; Deuteronomy 34:10), Moses had not seen him and could not make him known as Jesus, God's Son, "made him known" (John 1:18).

What About Us?

According to the Gospel of John, the greatest truth we can ever know is not truth about *something* but truth about *Someone*. Jesus is God; Jesus came to give a face to the divine. When we receive Jesus into our lives, we can live with new purpose, new power, and new peace.

QUESTIONS

1. Why is it important that Jesus be fully divine as well as human?

2. What do we say to people who can't understand how anybody can be completely human and completely divine?

3. What was the primary role of John the baptizer?

4. What are ways in which we can witness to people about who Jesus is?

Focal Text
John 2:1–22

Background
John 2

Main Idea
Jesus, God's Word to us, is superior to all other answers to our deepest needs.

Question to Explore
So *why* did Jesus turn the water into wine?

Study Aim
To contrast Jesus' superiority in meeting our deepest needs to other attempted solutions

Study and Action Emphases
- Affirm the Bible as our authoritative guide for life and ministry
- Share the gospel with all people
- Develop a growing, vibrant faith

LESSON TWO

Whatever Jesus Tells You

Quick Read
Jesus' turning the water into wine and challenging temple worship show the sufficiency and superiority of Jesus in contrast to Judaism and to all human attempts to find answers to our needs.

Who is Jesus? That's what the previous lesson on the first chapter of John told us. Jesus is divine, and he is the life, the light, and the Lamb of God. As the Son of God, Jesus called people to follow him. Along with these disciples, Jesus was now ready to embark on his ministry.

Who is Jesus? The answer to this question leads naturally into the emphasis of chapter 2 of John's Gospel. The second chapter of John contains two remarkable incidents in Jesus' life. First, he turned water into wine. Second, he turned over the tables in the temple. When we look carefully at these episodes in the ministry of Jesus, we see affirmed that Jesus is indeed the Son of God, and we see the difference that Jesus makes in human life. We see Jesus' superiority in meeting our deepest needs. Indeed, we see that Jesus is superior to all other attempts to meet these needs.

Jesus Turns Water into Wine (2:1–11)

The Gospel of John emphasizes the importance of what it calls *signs*. These signs were miracles that Jesus performed, but they were not designed to draw attention to themselves. They were signs pointing to Jesus as the Messiah and the fulfillment of Jewish religious expectations.

When I was a child, our family lived in Miami, Florida. Sometimes we visited relatives near Tampa. We drove old highway 41 through the Everglades. When we were about thirty miles from a little town called Clewiston, signs would start appearing advertising the Old South Barbeque House. "Only 30 minutes to Old South Barbeque;" "The Best Barbeque in the World;" "Only 10 miles to Finger-licking Barbeque." By the time we reached Clewiston, we were hungry. We pulled our car into the restaurant parking lot along with all the other cars.

We were drawn to the food by the signs. The signs were wonderfully effective, but we would have missed their purpose if we had not stopped at the place to which they were pointing.

The miracles or signs in the Gospel of John point to Jesus. The first sign happened in a small town in Galilee called Cana. Apparently Jesus knew the family who was having the wedding. He and his disciples had been invited. Jesus, his disciples, and his mother were all there.

In the first century, wedding celebrations could last a week. The host was expected to provide food and drink for everybody. Next time you hear the father of a bride complaining about the cost of his daughter's wedding, remind him about the fathers in the first century. Can you imagine all the

John 2:1–22

¹On the third day there was a wedding in Cana of Galilee, and the mother of Jesus was there. ²Jesus and his disciples had also been invited to the wedding. ³When the wine gave out, the mother of Jesus said to him, "They have no wine." ⁴And Jesus said to her, "Woman, what concern is that to you and to me? My hour has not yet come." ⁵His mother said to the servants, "Do whatever he tells you." ⁶Now standing there were six stone water jars for the Jewish rites of purification, each holding twenty or thirty gallons. ⁷Jesus said to them, "Fill the jars with water." And they filled them up to the brim. ⁸He said to them, "Now draw some out, and take it to the chief steward." So they took it. ⁹When the steward tasted the water that had become wine, and did not know where it came from (though the servants who had drawn the water knew), the steward called the bridegroom ¹⁰and said to him, "Everyone serves the good wine first, and then the inferior wine after the guests have become drunk. But you have kept the good wine until now." ¹¹Jesus did this, the first of his signs, in Cana of Galilee, and revealed his glory; and his disciples believed in him.

¹²After this he went down to Capernaum with his mother, his brothers, and his disciples; and they remained there a few days.

¹³The Passover of the Jews was near, and Jesus went up to Jerusalem. ¹⁴In the temple he found people selling cattle, sheep, and doves, and the money changers seated at their tables. ¹⁵Making a whip of cords, he drove all of them out of the temple, both the sheep and the cattle. He also poured out the coins of the money changers and overturned their tables. ¹⁶He told those who were selling the doves, "Take these things out of here! Stop making my Father's house a marketplace!" ¹⁷His disciples remembered that it was written, "Zeal for your house will consume me." ¹⁸The Jews then said to him, "What sign can you show us for doing this?" ¹⁹Jesus answered them, "Destroy this temple, and in three days I will raise it up." ²⁰The Jews then said, "This temple has been under construction for forty-six years, and will you raise it up in three days?" ²¹But he was speaking of the temple of his body. ²²After he was raised from the dead, his disciples remembered that he had said this; and they believed the scripture and the word that Jesus had spoken.

relatives, friends, and wedding party hanging around your house for a week? Plus you had to feed all of them.

A problem developed at the wedding in Cana. The wine ran out. When Jesus' mother came to ask for a miracle to replenish the wine, Jesus said, "Dear woman, why do you involve me? . . . My time has not yet come"

(John 2:4, NIV). Frankly, I wasn't allowed to talk to my mother like that. We need not see this manner of address as being unkind or insensitive, however. The situation is that Jesus' mother asked for more wine, and Jesus used this question to talk about his eternal significance.

When we take Jesus into our lives, we find that Jesus is the fulfillment of our longings, the joy for which our hearts yearn.

Jesus did what his mother asked, but the concern of this story isn't a wedding, wine, or a woman's request. These are part of the sign. The sign points to Jesus. Jesus is the new wine. To the Jews, wine symbolized the joy of new life. That's who Jesus is. He's the new life of God. When we take Jesus into our lives, we find that Jesus is the fulfillment of our longings, the joy for which our hearts yearn.

Several details about this miracle are important to note. First, Jesus told about his "hour" or time (2:4). According to the Gospel of John, three years remained in Jesus' life. Jesus knew where his life would end, however. He would give his life on a cross, and he would do it willingly. Nobody would make Jesus do it. Nobody would take his life. Jesus would give it because Jesus came to show people that he is God and that God loved them.

Sometimes we picture Jesus being taken to the cross against his will. Roman authorities, religious leaders, and soldiers seem to be in control. According to the Gospel of John, nothing is further from the truth. The Lamb of God willingly lay down his life for you and me.

A second important detail is the amount of new wine Jesus made. There were six water pots. Six is an incomplete Hebrew number. The religious faith of the Old Testament is fulfilled in the new wine of Jesus. Note the lavish love. Jesus filled six ceremonial water pots with wine, and each of the pots held twenty to thirty gallons. We are talking about a big celebration!

How sad when worship is marketed like some kind of entertainment and the focus on God is lost.

Have you ever been to one of those wedding receptions that serve "finger food"— celery stalks, carrot sticks, and small glasses of punch? The sandwiches may have been good, but they were small. In fact, while nobody was looking, you slipped five or six of those sandwiches into a napkin, hoping at some point you could go off by yourself and eat enough to make eating worthwhile. To make matters worse, you kept returning to the punchbowl for refills, and the server gave you the evil eye because she thought you were drinking more than your share.

The Temple

The temple in Jerusalem played a critical part in the worship of the Hebrew people. In fact, the temple was the center of their worship. For the Hebrew people, the temple was the place where God most fully dwelt.

The first Hebrew temple was built by Solomon, King David's son (2 Samuel 7:13; 1 Kings 6:2). Tragically, this temple was destroyed by Nebuchadnezzar in 587/586 BC. After the Jews returned from exile in Babylon about fifty years later, they rebuilt the temple. This second temple was finished in 515 BC (Ezra 6:15). Construction of the temple to which John 2 refers had been begun about 20 BC by King Herod.

The temple was the center of Jewish worship. When you and I think about this ancient building complex, we need to remember how vital this temple was to the Jewish people and how important the site continues to be to them.

When Jesus filled the six water pots, he symbolically placed himself as the fulfillment of the Jewish faith. He also underscored that the life and joy he brings us is beyond all our expectations. Some New Testament scholars suggest that the water Jesus turned to wine was actually from the well, since the word "draw" suggests drawing water from a well. Whether from the well or the six water pots, though, the important truth is that Jesus was showing his superiority to and fulfillment of Judaism in meeting human needs.

A third detail of this first sign that Jesus performed is also revealing. Affluent Jews hired a chief steward who was like the consummate wedding director. The steward took charge of all the wedding festivities. This allowed the parents, family, and friends to celebrate without having to worry about enough food and other details. So when Jesus had turned the water into wine, the servants brought the new wine for the steward to taste. "Everyone serves the good wine first," the steward told the bridegroom, "and then the inferior wine after the guests have become drunk. But you have kept the good wine until now" (2:10).

We are talking about a big celebration!

The lesson is straightforward. The faith of the Old Testament was a worthy faith. We learn so much in the Old Testament about how God works. People like Abraham, Sarah, David, Ruth, and countless others inspire us with the courage of their faith. However, as wonderful as the first thirty-nine books of the Bible are, the best was yet to come. Jesus came as God's best revelation (see Hebrews 1:1–2).

Jesus is the new wine. Jesus fulfills the expectations of the Old Testament for the Messiah and brings the most complete expression of divine love and life.

Jesus Overturns the Tables in the Temple (2:12–22)

After Jesus turned the water into wine, he traveled from Cana through Capernaum into the city of Jerusalem. The city was packed with Jewish pilgrims who had come to celebrate the feast of Passover. Celebrated in the spring, Passover was the annual remembrance by the Jews of how God had brought them from the bondage of Egypt. This was the Jewish exodus, the continuing reminder of how their God had saved and rescued them.

The Lamb of God willingly lay down his life for you and me.

When Jesus arrived at the temple in Jerusalem, he found people selling cattle, sheep, and doves. The moneychangers sat nearby. These religious pilgrims to Jerusalem couldn't bring their own animals long distances, and so they bought these animals to sacrifice. These pilgrims had the currencies of their own country. For a fee, the moneychangers were willing to exchange the pilgrims' money of another country for money that could be used to purchase animals in the temple.

This buying, selling, and charging did not make Jesus happy. In fact, John says he made a whip of cords, drove the merchants and their animals out of the temple, and then overturned the tables. Then Jesus told them (2:16), "Take these things out of here! Stop making my Father's house a marketplace!"

Jesus fulfills the expectations of the Old Testament for the Messiah and brings the most complete expression of divine love and life.

This account of Jesus' actions in the temple reminds us that some things demand our opposition. When worship, the very central component of our faith, is trivialized, we need to speak out. When the worship of the Living God becomes self-promotion, we need to say something. Amazing, isn't it, how the most beautiful things in life can be used and abused? Worship is a beautiful word. It represents the gift of ourselves to God. How sad when worship is marketed like some kind of entertainment and the focus on God is lost.

What Jesus did in the temple was more than the act itself; it was a sign. Jesus told the Jewish leaders, "Destroy this temple, and in three days I will raise it up" (2:19). The Jews looked at their beautiful temple and reminded Jesus that the building had been under construction for forty-six years. The irony is obvious. How was Jesus to build a temple like the one in Jerusalem in three days?

What the Jewish listeners didn't understand was that Jesus was still using the word "temple," but he had changed the meaning. Jesus was talking about a new home for worship, a new "building" that God was making where people would come to worship the God revealed in Jesus Christ. However, this new "building" was not a temple made by human hands. The temple was Jesus himself. When Jesus talked about destroying the temple and it being rebuilt in three days, he was talking about his own death and resurrection. The Gospel of John also tells that even the disciples of Jesus did not understand his deeper meaning until after his resurrection.

Jesus spoke about the eternal, and people were thinking only about the earthly.

I once knew a preacher who used to say often during a sermon, "Do you understand?" This minister wanted to know whether his listeners understood what he was saying. Some in the congregation would nod their heads; others would say "Amen"; and others would continue to stare into space.

Naturally, those of us who preach like to be understood. It's not a compliment for someone to leave the sanctuary on Sunday morning and say, "What you said seemed very theological, but I really didn't comprehend a thing."

In the Gospel of John, though, Jesus often spoke about profound things, and his listeners, including his disciples, did not understand. Part of the reason is that Jesus talked about the ways of God, and his hearers were focused only on what was in front of them. To put it another way,

The Church and the Building

When I lived in Louisville, Kentucky, a beautiful church building was destroyed by an arsonist's fire. Later the church members built another place where they could come for worship services. Many of the members commented, however, that the fire, although devastating, reminded them of the heart of worship.

Our temple as Christians is the God revealed in Jesus Christ. While having a place to worship is important, far more important is something else. We worship a Person, Jesus the Christ, and no arsonist can destroy that.

Jesus spoke about the eternal, and people were thinking only about the earthly.

That is one of the fascinating aspects of the Gospel of John. Some people only see an upset Jesus who did not want commerce to take place in the sanctuary. While we may not like the church to be the place where someone sells tapes and prayer cloths, that really is not the point of John 2. In John 2, Jesus is the divine one; he is the "new temple of God" where we meet and worship the God who calls us to give him our lives. While this "temple" named Jesus would be killed, his death wouldn't last long. The Jews had constructed their temple for forty-six years. On the third day, the new temple would arise, complete and alive.

Jesus is God's supreme answer for meeting our deepest needs.

What About Us?

We live in a world in which people often seek various answers other than Jesus for meeting their needs and dealing with their difficulties. They seek "practical" solutions involving money, people, business institutions, governmental institutions, and carefully-made plans. People in our world may even seek "spiritual" answers aimed at helping them "feel good" or at least feel better.

Often these answers have little if anything to do with Jesus. This lesson reminds us that such answers can be only partial answers if they are helpful at all. Only Jesus is sufficient for meeting our deepest needs. Indeed, Jesus is God's supreme answer for meeting our deepest needs.

QUESTIONS

1. What signs in your life have pointed you to Jesus as the Lord of your life?
2. Do we still have signs today? Can those signs be rather ordinary events or people, pointing us to the extraordinary life of Jesus the Christ?
3. What qualities of the way we live give evidence that we have the new life and new joy that Jesus brings?
4. What places have been crucial in your pilgrimage of faith?
5. What does it mean to worship the God revealed in Jesus Christ?

Focal Text

John 3:1–16

Background

John 3:1–21

Main Idea

In love and through Jesus, God offers eternal life to those willing for God to create them anew.

Question to Explore

How can anyone be born after having grown old?

Study Aim

To decide whether and to what extent I am willing for God to create me anew

Study and Action Emphases

- Affirm the Bible as our authoritative guide for life and ministry
- Share the gospel with all people
- Develop a growing, vibrant faith

LESSON THREE

For God So Loved

Quick Read

Jesus' conversation with Nicodemus shows us that even religious people need to allow God to create them anew. When we let God create us anew, the change is so great that it is like being reborn, but to a different kind of life—God's kind of life.

What do you believe? The theme of our lessons from the Gospel of John is, "So That You May Believe." But believe in what or believe in whom? The Gospel of John is very clear in its answer. Are you? Consider your answer as you study Jesus' conversation with a religious leader named Nicodemus.

The Conversation (3:1–10)

In John 3:1–10 Nicodemus is a key figure in a most important conversation with Jesus. Jesus had declared himself in chapter 2 as the fulfillment of the Jewish faith. It would have been only natural for the Jewish leadership to want to know more about who he was. Nicodemus was one of the most capable representatives of the Jewish leaders.

Although we have relatively little information about Nicodemus, the information we have lets us know that he was an impressive person. Nicodemus was a Pharisee. The Pharisees were the most dominant group in first-century Judaism. Known for their strict adherence to Jewish law, the Pharisees represented a faith that took both God and religious practices very seriously.

Nicodemus was also a "leader of the Jews" (3:1). This probably meant that he was a member of the Sanhedrin. Seventy of the most respected Jewish men were selected to be members of the Sanhedrin. This was the Jewish high court, roughly akin to the Supreme Court of the United States. The members of the Sanhedrin were chosen because of their moral stature, their knowledge of the law, and their abilities to make prudent decisions.

The Gospel of John indicates that Nicodemus came to Jesus at night. Since John does not tell us why this meeting was at night, speculation has run rampant. Was Nicodemus the official representative of the Jewish hierarchy sent to investigate Jesus' religious credentials, and did he thus come at night because the Jewish leadership did not want other people to think that they were in any way associated with Jesus? Or did Nicodemus come on a personal quest, having a religious faith but looking for something to fill the empty vacuum at the center of his life but not wanting others to know of his search?

While such speculation is intriguing, the fact is that we do not know why Nicodemus came at night. What we do know is that he was polite to Jesus. Nicodemus referred to Jesus as "Rabbi," and added, "we know you

John 3:1–16

¹Now there was a Pharisee named Nicodemus, a leader of the Jews. ²He came to Jesus by night and said to him, "Rabbi, we know that you are a teacher who has come from God; for no one can do these signs that you do apart from the presence of God." ³Jesus answered him, "Very truly, I tell you, no one can see the kingdom of God without being born from above." ⁴Nicodemus said to him, "How can anyone be born after having grown old? Can one enter a second time into the mother's womb and be born?" ⁵Jesus answered, "Very truly, I tell you, no one can enter the kingdom of God without being born of water and Spirit. ⁶What is born of the flesh is flesh, and what is born of the Spirit is spirit. ⁷Do not be astonished that I said to you, 'You must be born from above.' ⁸The wind blows where it chooses, and you hear the sound of it, but you do not know where it comes from or where it goes. So it is with everyone who is born of the Spirit." ⁹Nicodemus said to him, "How can these things be?" ¹⁰Jesus answered him, "Are you a teacher of Israel, and yet you do not understand these things?

¹¹"Very truly, I tell you, we speak of what we know and testify to what we have seen; yet you do not receive our testimony. ¹²If I have told you about earthly things and you do not believe, how can you believe if I tell you about heavenly things? ¹³No one has ascended into heaven except the one who descended from heaven, the Son of Man. ¹⁴And just as Moses lifted up the serpent in the wilderness, so must the Son of Man be lifted up, ¹⁵that whoever believes in him may have eternal life.

¹⁶"For God so loved the world that he gave his only Son, so that everyone who believes in him may not perish but may have eternal life."

are a teacher who has come from God; for no one can do these signs that you do apart from the presence of God" (3:3).

To call Jesus a rabbi was an extraordinary compliment. Rabbis were the best-trained, most skillful of all Jewish teachers. Being a rabbi can be compared to having tenure as a full professor at a prestigious university. Referring to Jesus as rabbi is especially startling since Jesus apparently had no formal education. He didn't even have an *honorary* doctorate! Jesus had come from Galilee to Jerusalem, but apparently his reputation as a miracle worker had preceded him.

We also know from John 3 that Jesus really did not want to talk to Nicodemus about educational credentials, teaching ability, or any other earthly matter. Immediately, Jesus turned the conversation to eternal matters. The essence of Jesus' message is that Nicodemus, no matter what his earthly stature was, must be "born from above" (3:3).

Some translations of the Bible render the two Greek words translated "born from above" as "born again" (KJV, NIV, NASB). The words can be translated either way, and the message is similar in either case. What Jesus was saying to Nicodemus is what Jesus says to all of us: *God loves us. We are not saved by what we achieve. We come to God to receive the gift of new birth and new life.*

> A message about receiving love is often more difficult to understand and accept than a message about achieving love.

The rest of the conversation between Jesus and Nicodemus indicates that at this point in his life Nicodemus did not understand this incredible "gift love" of God. It's easy to be critical of Nicodemus. He was a very bright person. Nicodemus had not made it to where he was in life without being perceptive and discerning. Yet, he was unable to fathom what Jesus was saying. When Jesus spoke about the birth from above being like the wind, the message blew right by Nicodemus. A message about receiving love is often more difficult to understand and accept than a message about achieving love.

When I was in fourth grade at Fairlawn Elementary School in Miami, Florida, I had the infamous Miss Taylor as my teacher. She made sure that we students understood that her name was *Miss* Taylor. From our nine- and ten-year-old perspectives, those of us in the class wondered how anybody could live with her. Miss Taylor was stern, demanding, and made us work for every grade.

> Not only do we live forever in the presence of God but also we live now, knowing that Jesus the Christ is with us to give us strength for whatever we face.

I remember the grading system. *E* was excellent; *S* was satisfactory; and *U* meant that you had the questionable pleasure of spending another year with Miss Taylor in fourth grade. Our teacher pounded into us that we had to work hard and earn good grades. I can't imagine going to Miss Taylor to say, "I haven't earned an *E*, but I know that you are gracious, kind, and loving." I would have ended up in the "time-out chair" or probably something worse.

Miss Taylor's philosophy permeated most of what I learned as a child. I learned that you get what you earn, you achieve what you work for, and there is no such thing as a "free lunch." If you wanted to make an *E* in Arithmetic, you had to study for the tests and perform well on them. As

Pharisee

Nicodemus was a Pharisee. Pharisees in the first century were very prominent in Jewish society and religion. The New Testament tends to cast the Pharisees as enemies of Jesus.

While the meaning of the name *Pharisee* is somewhat uncertain, it may mean *separate ones*. Since the Jews were under Roman rule, the Pharisees tried to preserve the uniqueness of their Hebrew faith. They were devoted to traditions that helped them to live in a way that they believed was faithful to Judaism.

Among the religious emphases that the Pharisees stressed were ritual purity and strict observance of the Sabbath laws and other rules. We can see how these allegiances created conflict between the Pharisees and Jesus. Jesus seemed to be less concerned about strict observance of some laws. To the Pharisees this was a threat because their identity as Jews was intricately woven into a strict observance of Jewish traditions.

---

students, we were taught to work hard and to achieve. Implicitly we even learned that much of life was competing with one another.

Therefore, I can hardly blame Nicodemus for misunderstanding Jesus. After all, this Pharisee had studied the religious law, lived by its tenets, and was successful in achieving a status that very few attained. I'm sure that the teachers of Nicodemus pointed to him as an example of what can happen to a student who works hard.

The problem was that Jesus was talking a different language. Like the temple episode prior to this, Jesus was using words in a different way. To Jesus, our relationship with God is built on *receiving* God's love. We may do good works, but those works are done as an expression of a love we have freely received. The problem with Nicodemus wasn't that he was not a good person. Nicodemus was very good. What he lacked was that relationship to God that comes when we freely open ourselves to the wind of God and we come to know that we are loved unconditionally by God.

Jesus is absolutely unique and different from every other person who has ever lived.

Frankly, Nicodemus represents the way I have thought about life and have done life. I am so conditioned by an environment that has said, *Be good and do well.* In following that command, perhaps you will be loved by others, but, even if you are not, at least others will respect you because of your hard work. How liberating if Nicodemus had seen that he was loved by God not because he was a Pharisee or a ruler of the Jews. He was loved just because he was Nicodemus.

Before moving to the next section of Scripture, consider a detail found in verse 5. In that verse, Jesus referred to the need to be "born of water and Spirit." What did he mean? Nicodemus might well have known of the Old Testament connection between water and the coming of the Spirit (see Ezekiel 36:25–27). In addition, ideas swirled about in the religious scene of Nicodemus's day that connected water and spirit. Furthermore, the first readers of the Gospel of John might well have thought of Christian baptism when "water" was mentioned. Note that in this entire passage Jesus used various expressions to refer to genuine spiritual experience. He spoke of seeing "the kingdom of God" (3:3); being "born from above" (3:3, 7); entering "the kingdom of God" (3:5); being "born of water and Spirit" (3:5); being "born of the Spirit" (3:6); and "having eternal life" (3:15, 16). Although the details and emphases of each expression vary, these basically are parallel expressions for the experience of salvation.

> *What is most critical to Jesus and to us is whether we believe that Jesus is God and whether we receive personally the message that Jesus was born, lived, died, and was raised on the third day so that we may "have eternal life" (John 3:15).*

The Message (3:11–16)

Nicodemus appears two more times in John's Gospel (7:50; 19:39). For now, though, he disappears from view. To me, Jesus did all the speaking through 3:21, although some quite reputable Bible students suggest that at

"For God So Loved the World"

What is love? The Greek language had several words for love, two of which appear in the New Testament.

Phileo is brotherly or sisterly love. It may mean love for a friend.

Phileo is a strong kind of love, but it is nothing like *agape* love. *Agape* is another Greek word for love. John used the verb form of this word to describe God's love toward us. *Agape* is the kind of love that seeks nothing in return from the one who is loved. *Agape* seeks only the best for the one who is loved. *Agape* cannot be earned. We receive this love as a free gift from God.

some point in these verses the words of Jesus end and we have the reflections of the writer of the Gospel of John. It's probably not fair to call Jesus' monologue a sermon. It's not as long as most sermons, and the words are not part of a worship event. Most New Testament scholars refer to Jesus' message as a soliloquy. Whatever we call 3:11–21, we recognize that it contains memorable and life-altering words.

To believe in Jesus is to commit our lives to him.

The message begins with the acknowledgment that Jesus' message is heavenly or eternal in the sense that Jesus is speaking about matters he has seen (3:11–12). Since Jesus is divine as well as human, he talked about God the Father with the familiarity of first-hand experience.

Verse 13 speaks about Jesus' ascending and descending between this world and heaven. This verse refers to Jesus as the Son of Man, a title that would have communicated his divine status to John's readers. The ascending and descending describe the incarnation of God in Jesus. The message is that no one else is like Jesus. Jesus is absolutely unique and different from every other person who has ever lived. He has been sent by God to this earth for a mission. Jesus descended from his heavenly prerogatives. A part of his living among us involved his death.

The reference to the Son of Man being "lifted up" on a cross draws an analogy to the Old Testament patriarch Moses, who lifted up the serpent in the wilderness (3:14–15; see Numbers 21:4–9). What is most critical to Jesus and to us is whether we believe that Jesus is God and whether we receive personally the message that Jesus was born, lived, died, and was raised on the third day so that we may "have eternal life" (John 3:15).

God's love prompted God to give us the best gift.

Once again the Gospel of John returns to one of its favorite themes, "eternal life" (3:15). Think about what Jesus said. To receive the love of God in Jesus Christ is to receive a new life. Not only do we live forever in the presence of God but also we live now, knowing that Jesus the Christ is with us to give us strength for whatever we face.

The story is told of a man who wanted to be buried in his solid gold Cadillac. When the day of his funeral came, the man was propped up at the wheel of the Cadillac with his white-gloved hands fixed on the steering wheel. As the crane lowered the gold Cadillac and the man into the grave, a bystander remarked, "Man, that's really living!" Amazing, isn't it, how we can be misled about what will bring us life?

John 3:16 is undoubtedly the best-known verse in the Bible for many Christians. Many have referred to this verse as *the little gospel.* Since *gospel* means *good news,* John 3:16 is incredibly good news. In fact, this verse contains the best news of all.

Amazing, isn't it, how we can be misled about what will bring us life?

First, we are reminded that God loves the world. When I was a child, I used to sing, "Red and yellow, black and white, They are precious in His sight."[1] It's not true to say that God has no favorites. What we have to say is that no matter who we are, what we have done, or how we've succeeded or failed, we are all God's favorites.

Second, God's love prompted God to give us the best gift. God gave us Jesus. The Greek words translated "his only Son" really mean *God's unique, one of a kind, never to be repeated, Son.* In other words, God loved us so much that God sent us his best.

To receive the love of God in Jesus Christ is to receive a new life.

Third, however, we have to believe this truth in order to have eternal life. In the Bible, to believe in Jesus is more than to acknowledge in our heads that Jesus is God's gift. The root of the word "belief" is *lief,* which is the word from which we get the term, *life.* To believe in Jesus is to commit our lives to him. When we do that, we can know with full assurance that we have eternal life.

What About Us?

For real love to happen, there must be a relationship. I don't love in the abstract. I love my wife, my children, my friends, and people who have touched my life. Similarly, God calls us into a relationship with him. God gives us his very life to show his love. The question now is: *Do we give God our lives to show God how much we love him?*

QUESTIONS

1. In your life, what factors or people helped you to understand that you needed to be born from above?

2. What did you say to God when you understood God's love and sacrifice for you?

3. Since God loves the world, what does that mean for Americans as we view people in the world whom we consider our enemies?

4. What do you think was going on in God the Father's heart when he sent his Son to the world knowing that his Son would be killed?

5. If we tell a person that he or she needs to "believe in Jesus," what do we mean by those words?

NOTES

1. "Jesus Loves the Little Children," words by Geo. F. Root.

Focal Text

John 4:4–30, 39–42

Background

John 4:1–42

Main Idea

Jesus crosses all human barriers to invite all people into intimate relationship with God and with one another.

Question to Explore

What's keeping you from Jesus—or from telling others about him?

Study Aim

To decide on ways I will follow Jesus' example in crossing the human barriers that separate people from God and one another

Study and Action Emphases

- Affirm the Bible as our authoritative guide for life and ministry
- Share the gospel with all people
- Develop a growing, vibrant faith
- Include all God's family in decision-making and service
- Value all people as created in the image of God
- Obey and serve Jesus by meeting physical, spiritual, and emotional needs

LESSON FOUR  If You Knew the Gift of God

Quick Read

Jesus' willingness to accept the Samaritan woman shows how intent he was on crossing human barriers to enter into relationship with people. What Jesus did helps us know how willing he is to enter into relationship with us and challenges us to relate to other people in the way he did.

43

Recently I was in another city to preach a revival. I went to a store to buy a gift for my wife. Whenever I'm out of town, I like to buy something I can give her when I come home. These gifts are an expression of the love I have for my wife.

Suppose I chose somebody I didn't know or maybe didn't even like that much and bought that person a gift. What if this person were a coworker who gets under my skin? What if this person were a neighbor who is loud? What if it were somebody who had done something to hurt me and who had never apologized?

It's easy to give to someone we love. But what about giving to the person who has never given us anything but trouble and grief? In John 4, we find a beautiful example of the breadth of God's love.

Receiving the Gift (4:4–26)

Most of the time that Jesus spoke about the love of God he did so in the ordinary movements of his life. Jesus didn't wait until he found a synagogue on the Sabbath day to talk about God. Neither did Jesus have a set time during the week that was designated for visitation or for evangelism. In the normal traffic patterns of his life, Jesus shared with people that God loved them and that Jesus himself was the consummate gift of that love.

We find Jesus on the move in this text. With his disciples, Jesus was traveling from the province of Judea in the southern part of the nation to Galilee in the northern part (John 4:3). Samaria was between Judea and Galilee. The Gospel of John says that for Jesus to make the trip, "he had to go through Samaria" (4:4). Actually, in one sense, Jesus didn't have to go through Samaria. He could have chosen another way. That was the most direct route, but many Jews would go out of their way to avoid Samaria because they despised the Samaritans.

Why was it that Jesus "had to go through Samaria" (4:4)? The implication of John's Gospel is that God was leading his Son and it was important that the gift of divine love be offered to everybody (see John 3:16).

Jesus went to Jacob's well in the city of Sychar. There he met a Samaritan woman. Only Jesus and the woman were at the well. The disciples had gone into the city to buy provisions for the trip to Galilee. At the well, Jesus said to the woman, "Give me a drink" (4:7). Those words set off a conversation that reveals both who the woman was and who Jesus is.

John 4:4–30, 39–42

⁴But he had to go through Samaria. ⁵So he came to a Samaritan city called Sychar, near the plot of ground that Jacob had given to his son Joseph. ⁶Jacob's well was there, and Jesus, tired out by his journey, was sitting by the well. It was about noon.

⁷A Samaritan woman came to draw water, and Jesus said to her, "Give me a drink." ⁸(His disciples had gone to the city to buy food.) ⁹The Samaritan woman said to him, "How is it that you, a Jew, ask a drink of me, a woman of Samaria?" (Jews do not share things in common with Samaritans.) ¹⁰Jesus answered her, "If you knew the gift of God, and who it is that is saying to you, 'Give me a drink,' you would have asked him, and he would have given you living water." ¹¹The woman said to him, "Sir, you have no bucket, and the well is deep. Where do you get that living water? ¹²Are you greater than our ancestor Jacob, who gave us the well, and with his sons and his flocks drank from it?" ¹³Jesus said to her, "Everyone who drinks of this water will be thirsty again, ¹⁴but those who drink of the water that I will give them will never be thirsty. The water that I will give will become in them a spring of water gushing up to eternal life." ¹⁵The woman said to him, "Sir, give me this water, so that I may never be thirsty or have to keep coming here to draw water."

¹⁶Jesus said to her, "Go, call your husband, and come back." ¹⁷The woman answered him, "I have no husband." Jesus said to her, "You are right in saying, 'I have no husband'; ¹⁸for you have had five husbands, and the one you have now is not your husband. What you have said is true!" ¹⁹The woman said to him, "Sir, I see that you are a prophet. ²⁰Our ancestors worshiped on this mountain, but you say that the place where people must worship is in Jerusalem." ²¹Jesus said to her, "Woman, believe me, the hour is coming when you will worship the Father neither on this mountain nor in Jerusalem. ²²You worship what you do not know; we worship what we know, for salvation is from the Jews. ²³But the hour is coming, and is now here, when the true worshipers will worship the Father in spirit and truth, for the Father seeks such as these to worship him. ²⁴God is spirit, and those who worship him must worship in spirit and truth." ²⁵The woman said to him, "I know that Messiah is coming" (who is called Christ). "When he comes, he will proclaim all things to us." ²⁶Jesus said to her, "I am he, the one who is speaking to you."

²⁷Just then his disciples came. They were astonished that he was speaking with a woman, but no one said, "What do you want?" or, "Why are you speaking with her?" ²⁸Then the woman left her water jar and

went back to the city. She said to the people, ²⁹"Come and see a man who told me everything I have ever done! He cannot be the Messiah, can he?" ³⁰They left the city and were on their way to him.

³⁹Many Samaritans from that city believed in him because of the woman's testimony, "He told me everything I have ever done." ⁴⁰So when the Samaritans came to him, they asked him to stay with them; and he stayed there two days. ⁴¹And many more believed because of his word. ⁴²They said to the woman, "It is no longer because of what you said that we believe, for we have heard for ourselves, and we know that this is truly the Savior of the world."

Who was the woman at the well? Because she came alone to draw water in the middle of the day, she was isolated from the other women of the town. Later conversation with Jesus revealed that she already had five husbands and she was now living with a man who wasn't her husband (4:16–18). To put it plainly, this woman was living in an immoral manner. Thus she was separated from the "good women" of Sychar who didn't want to be seen with her.

It's easy to give to someone we love. But what about giving to the person who has never given us anything but trouble and grief?

Not only was her morality questionable, but also she was a woman. Unfortunately, in the first century, women often were regarded as little more than property. A man and a woman simply were not seen talking in public, especially a single man like Jesus and a woman of questionable reputation.

Not only was she a woman of questionable morality, but also she was a Samaritan. While the Samaritans and the Jews had the same heritage, they viewed each other with suspicion. In fact, the Jews considered the Samaritans half-breeds and infidels.

In many ways, this Samaritan woman represents a striking contrast to Nicodemus. Nobody would have questioned the morals of Nicodemus. He was the ideal Jew. On the other hand, the Samaritan woman was on the opposite end of the spectrum.

Yet, both the woman and Nicodemus had one thing in common. They both needed to receive the gift of God.

The message of John is clear. Whether we are moral or immoral, good or bad in the eyes of society, we all need to receive the gift of God.

Furthermore, neither our gender nor our racial or cultural background stands in the way.

This raises the question, *Who is Jesus?* If we know that the woman needs love that she has apparently never found in a human relationship, who then is this "new man in her life"? Can Jesus show the Samaritan woman what God's unconditional love is?

The conversation at the well revolved around the theme of water. Amazingly, Jesus took what was at hand and turned it into a message about the "living water" (4:10).

In the normal traffic patterns of his life, Jesus shared with people that God loved them and that Jesus himself was the consummate gift of that love.

Characteristic of John's Gospel, the woman and Jesus talked about water at two levels. She thought of water as the drink that came from the well. However, Jesus used "living water" as an image of what he gives that quenches the spiritual thirst of people's lives (4:10).

The woman's recognizing who Jesus was seems to have been a gradual process. When Jesus finished talking about "living water," she asked for that kind of water so she wouldn't have to return to the well. Then Jesus told the woman about her not-so-impressive marital track record. She was astounded. Jesus knew something she hadn't revealed, and now the Samaritan woman confessed, "Sir, I see that you are a prophet" (4:19).

Samaria

When Jesus traveled from Judea to Galilee, he traveled through the area of Samaria. Samaria was a district located in the central hill country of Palestine.

While the Jews shared a common heritage ("our ancestor Jacob," 4:12), they also shared an enmity toward each other. The origin of this intense dislike is difficult to trace. Likely the dislike relates to the fact that the Jews considered the Samaritans to be "half-breeds," not fully Jews. According to 2 Kings 17:17–24, the king of Assyria had brought people from various parts of the Assyrian Empire to settle Samaria after the defeat of the Northern Kingdom in the eighth century BC.

Religious differences also separated the Jews and the Samaritans. The Samaritans regarded Mount Gerizim, not Jerusalem, as the center for the worship of God. Also, the Samaritans accepted only the Pentateuch, the first five books of the Old Testament, as sacred Scripture. The Samaritans maintained that they, not the Jews, were the preservers and bearers of the true faith of the Old Testament.

Jesus had moved in her eyes from being simply a Jewish man to being a prophet.

The opening of this woman's eyes parallels some of our own conversion experiences. Some people, like the Apostle Paul, have a cataclysmic conversion experience. In a moment's time, everything in life is reversed. One moment Paul despised and persecuted Christians. On the road to Damascus, however, every priority was radically reversed for him.

> Whether we are moral or immoral, good or bad in the eyes of society, we all need to receive the gift of God.

Others of us come to Jesus more gradually. We never despised him, but over a period of time we began to understand that Jesus was more than a Jewish man of the first century. Perhaps we were impressed by his teachings. Maybe we were drawn to Jesus' care for the oppressed and the downtrodden. Or, as was the Samaritan woman, perhaps we were struck by the insight Jesus had into our lives and by the sense that Jesus offered us healing for our brokenness.

The woman tried to engage Jesus in discussing the proper place for worship—Jerusalem or Mount Gerizim in Samaria—which was a bone of contention between Jews and Samaritans. Jesus replied that genuine worship went beyond such a matter (4:21, 23). Then, because the Samaritan faith was similar in some respects to that of the Jews, this woman was also looking for the Messiah to come and attempted to move the conversation in that direction. In response,

> We change our behavior because God changes our being.

Jesus continued to reveal himself to the Samaritan woman. The climax of Jesus' revelation to her came when the woman said that she was waiting for the Messiah (4:25). "I am he," Jesus replied, "the one who is speaking to you" (4:26).

While the woman didn't respond with an overwhelmingly positive statement of faith, we do know from later verses that her life was changed. Much like us, she still needed to be clearer about who Jesus really was and about the power of the gift she had received.

Forty-seven years after my conversion experience, I still find myself growing in areas of my life that need to be given to Jesus as Lord. That's the nature of our faith. Just as Jesus was on a journey, so our salvation experience is the beginning of a journey in which we grow to understand more who Jesus is and to surrender more completely our lives to him as Lord.

Sharing the Gift (4:27–30)

Just as Jesus was telling the woman that he is the Messiah, the disciples returned from the city. The Gospel of John lets its readers know that the disciples were "astonished" that he was talking to a woman (4:27). At least the disciples had the good sense to keep their astonishment to themselves.

After this one-verse interlude, the spotlight focuses again on the woman at the well. She was so moved by what Jesus had told her that she left her water jar at the well and returned to the city. The woman told everyone (4:29), "Come and see a man who told me everything I have ever done! He cannot be the Messiah, can he?"

This strange confession of faith seems to indicate that the woman had made another step in the direction of understanding who Jesus is. First she was awed that Jesus knew

What if we say we have no doubts about who Jesus is but seldom, if ever, tell anybody outside our Sunday School class how Jesus can change a life?

all about her. Probably what amazed her wasn't only that Jesus *saw* her for who she was but that Jesus *loved* her for who she was. This man knew all about her failures, her brokenness, her search for love, her multiple marriages, and her present life with a man to whom she was not married.

How did Jesus treat her? Did he condemn her? Did Jesus tell her to straighten up her life and then she could accept God's gift of love? While it is apparent that Jesus didn't approve of her lifestyle, Jesus understood that none of us can really be different unless God is making us different. We change our behavior because God changes our being.

After the woman had told the people that Jesus knew all about her, she expressed her faith in a question that reflects hope (4:29), "He cannot be the Messiah, can he?" Perhaps we might like for her profession of faith to be more positive and direct. Let's give her the credit she deserves, though. She did tell people about Jesus, and those people went to see him. What if we say we have no doubts about who Jesus is but seldom, if ever, tell anybody outside our Sunday School class how Jesus can change a life? Also, this woman had the courage to tell *everybody*, even the men of her

Mount Gerizim

A primary difference between the Jews and the Samaritans was the place they perceived as the center of worship. For the Jews it was the temple in Jerusalem. The Samaritans considered Mount Gerizim to be the most sacred of all places.

Mount Gerizim is about 2800 feet above sea level and is located in the central Samaritan highlands. In the fourth century BC, the Samaritans built their own temple on the top of Mount Gerizim.

The animosity between the Jews and the Samaritans shows again how important "places" are to Semitic people. Much of the current enmity in the Middle East between the Jews and the Palestinians can be traced to an intense desire for a homeland and for a place.

---

city. We don't even know this woman's name. She is simply the Samaritan woman at the well. Her reputation was soiled. Undoubtedly she had been disappointed many times in her life. Her relationship with men wasn't the healthiest. Yet, after spending just a portion of the day with Jesus, she gave a stronger witness than Nicodemus did.

Why was it that Jesus "had to go through Samaria" (4:4)?

Whatever the Samaritan woman said or however she said it, her words had an impact. The people of her city raced out to see Jesus. This unnamed woman had been given the gifts of life and hope. She gave to others what she had been given.

Knowing the Best Gift (4:39–42)

When I was twelve years old, I accepted Jesus as my Savior and Lord. My pastor, who died several years ago, was not a well-known preacher. To my knowledge, he was never elected as anything more than perhaps moderator of the local Baptist association. Yet, because of his faithful witness, the lives of many young people were touched, and an unusually large percentage of us have been in some kind of ministry.

The Samaritan woman was faithful. Maybe she never made it into any first-century "Who's Who." What she did as a witness, however, changed a city.

Some came to Jesus because of her testimony. Many came to Jesus after the people invited him to town and he shared with them the words of life.

Some people wanted it known that they were not brought to faith by the woman's words but by hearing Jesus himself.

It hardly seems to matter who gets the credit, though. In fact, when people come to know the best gift, the gift of life and love in Jesus Christ, it doesn't make any difference who is preaching, teaching, or giving a witness. What matters is that people's lives are changed by the Spirit of God. We can say the words or do something to let a person know that God loves him or her, but it is God who gives the gift.

> . . . *Our salvation experience is the beginning of a journey in which we grow to understand more who Jesus is and to surrender more completely our lives to him as Lord.*

We can help others to want that gift, however. We can tell them how God's giving us Jesus Christ is changing us and how God can touch their lives. That's the beauty of the life of this Samaritan woman at the well. She wasn't the most outstanding citizen of Sychar. In fact, she was an outcast or close to it. When she found the "living water," though, she wanted everyone to drink from the well.

QUESTIONS

1. Can you think of someone you see almost every day who needs you to tell what Jesus Christ is doing in your life?

2. Has God ever used an unexpected person to teach you about his love?

3. Why do you think the Gospel of John never tells us the woman's name? What name would you give her?

4. If you had been one of the disciples, would you have been astonished that Jesus was talking to a different kind of person from them?

5. Why do you think so many people responded to the woman's testimony? Was it what she said, the way her life had changed, or something else?

Focal Text

John 5:1–24, 31–40

Background

John 4:43—5:47

Main Idea

esus as God's Son has the authority to offer life in its fullness.

Question to Explore

Why do you believe in Jesus?

Study Aim

To identify reasons for believing in Jesus

Study and Action Emphases

- Affirm the Bible as our authoritative guide for life and ministry
- Share the gospel with all people
- Develop a growing, vibrant faith

LESSON FIVE

The Case for Jesus

Quick Read

Believing in Jesus is based on faith, not on reasoning. Reason seeks evidence, but faith calls for decision. Nevertheless, reasons and evidence can help to lead us to take the leap of faith.

Have you ever said, *If I could have seen one miracle that Jesus performed in the New Testament, I could convince everybody to believe he is the Son of God?* There's a problem with this logic. In John's Gospel some people saw and heard what Jesus did but still didn't believe.

Reason can help lead a person to the place where he or she takes the leap of faith. This passage of Scripture calls us to consider various pieces of evidence that can help lead to faith. In the final analysis, though, it's a matter of trusting faith.

A Strange Healing (5:1–9a)

Miracles are signs, and as such they must be interpreted. In John 5, Jesus came back to Jerusalem. Jesus headed for the temple to celebrate a Jewish festival. However, on the way he saw a number of people who were around a pool near what is known as "the Sheep Gate" (5:2). The Gospel of John underscores the despair of the scene by describing their conditions—"blind, lame, and paralyzed" (5:3). These people evidently had been brought by their friends or family to this place because they had no other hope. The legend of the pool was that sometimes when the water was stirred up, the first one into the pool was healed (5:7).

Jesus focused on one man at the pool. The Gospel of John says the man had been ill for thirty-eight years (5:5). Jesus knew he had been there a long time (5:6). What is being emphasized is the apparent hopeless condition of this man.

Jesus asked the man (5:6), "Do you want to be made well?" Why did Jesus ask that? Can't we assume that someone who is sick wants to get better? That would seem so. Consider other possibilities, though. Had the man at the pool learned to like his illness? After all, being sick can get us out of a lot of things. Let's face it: Sometimes at least some folks enjoy the attention that sickness brings them.

I had a student who was missing more than the allowed number of classes. He always had a reason—my stomach aches, my head hurts, I feel as if I'm getting a cold, my allergies are acting up, etc. He didn't have any major problems—just a litany of fairly minor problems. The student went to the doctor, and the physical examination showed a few minor problems like seasonal allergies.

At first, I excused the student. "I understand," I said. "I don't feel well either when I have a headache."

John 5:1–24, 31–40

¹After this there was a festival of the Jews, and Jesus went up to Jerusalem.

²Now in Jerusalem by the Sheep Gate there is a pool, called in Hebrew Beth-zatha, which has five porticoes. ³In these lay many invalids—blind, lame, and paralyzed. ⁵One man was there who had been ill for thirty-eight years. ⁶When Jesus saw him lying there and knew that he had been there a long time, he said to him, "Do you want to be made well?" ⁷The sick man answered him, "Sir, I have no one to put me into the pool when the water is stirred up; and while I am making my way, someone else steps down ahead of me." ⁸Jesus said to him, "Stand up, take your mat and walk." ⁹At once the man was made well, and he took up his mat and began to walk.

Now that day was a sabbath. ¹⁰So the Jews said to the man who had been cured, "It is the sabbath; it is not lawful for you to carry your mat." ¹¹But he answered them, "The man who made me well said to me, 'Take up your mat and walk.'" ¹²They asked him, "Who is the man who said to you, 'Take it up and walk'?" ¹³Now the man who had been healed did not know who it was, for Jesus had disappeared in the crowd that was there. ¹⁴Later Jesus found him in the temple and said to him, "See, you have been made well! Do not sin any more, so that nothing worse happens to you." ¹⁵The man went away and told the Jews that it was Jesus who had made him well. ¹⁶Therefore the Jews started persecuting Jesus, because he was doing such things on the sabbath. ¹⁷But Jesus answered them, "My Father is still working, and I also am working." ¹⁸For this reason the Jews were seeking all the more to kill him, because he was not only breaking the sabbath, but was also calling God his own Father, thereby making himself equal to God.

¹⁹Jesus said to them, "Very truly, I tell you, the Son can do nothing on his own, but only what he sees the Father doing; for whatever the Father does, the Son does likewise. ²⁰The Father loves the Son and shows him all that he himself is doing; and he will show him greater works than these, so that you will be astonished. ²¹Indeed, just as the Father raises the dead and gives them life, so also the Son gives life to whomever he wishes. ²²The Father judges no one but has given all judgment to the Son, ²³so that all may honor the Son just as they honor the Father. Anyone who does not honor the Son does not honor the Father who sent him. ²⁴Very truly, I tell you, anyone who hears my word and believes him who sent me has eternal life, and does not come under judgment, but has passed from death to life.

30"I can do nothing on my own. As I hear, I judge; and my judgment is just, because I seek to do not my own will but the will of him who sent me.

31"If I testify about myself, my testimony is not true. 32There is another who testifies on my behalf, and I know that his testimony to me is true. 33You sent messengers to John, and he testified to the truth. 34Not that I accept such human testimony, but I say these things so that you may be saved. 35He was a burning and shining lamp, and you were willing to rejoice for a while in his light. 36But I have a testimony greater than John's. The works that the Father has given me to complete, the very works that I am doing, testify on my behalf that the Father has sent me. 37And the Father who sent me has himself testified on my behalf. You have never heard his voice or seen his form, 38and you do not have his word abiding in you, because you do not believe him whom he has sent.

39"You search the scriptures because you think that in them you have eternal life; and it is they that testify on my behalf. 40Yet you refuse to come to me to have life.

After the student had been absent a number of times, I wondered whether I was doing him a favor. This young man was preparing to be a minister. Ministers understand that there are Sundays when you don't feel on top of your game, but you preach anyway. I told the student, "Unless you have a fever or are contagious, you will be in class."

Perhaps we can understand Jesus' question like this: *Could it be that you have become so used to your condition that you really don't want to change?* Or perhaps Jesus was saying to the man, *Right now you don't have to choose where you will go. You go where others take you. Being able to walk will make you have to decide where your feet will take you. Are you ready for that?*

This sign points not to the man who was healed but to Jesus who heals each of us in different ways.

Whatever the reason, Jesus asked the man (5:6), "Do you want to be made well?" The man really didn't answer. He told Jesus that nobody ever helped him into the pool when the water was stirred. Jesus said (5:8), "Stand up, take your mat and walk." The Gospel of John states, "At once, the man was made well, and he took up his mat and began to walk" (5:9). Jesus didn't need to put the man in the pool. Jesus' word was enough. Thirty-eight years of illness, and with a word from Jesus the man was made well.

This is high drama. Hopelessness is broken with a word from Jesus. A miracle happens.

Please understand that I don't want to rain on the parade of this story or spoil the party, but a couple of things need to be said. First, not everybody at the pool was healed even though Jesus was there. This needs to be said because some well-intentioned or not so well-intentioned preachers are teaching that Jesus wants everybody to be physically well. According to these preachers, the issue is our faith. If we have enough, Jesus will make us well. Tumors will be shrunk, cancers will be removed, and wheelchairs can be thrown away. If you and I just have enough faith, Jesus will make us well.

What we have in this miracle is not so much a story about human faith but an account of the divine Jesus who possesses the power to change lives.

Think about this for just a minute. What if you are the person who is not healed? Does this mean you lack faith? Ruby Jones and her daughter, Ruby Fern Jones, were members of the church I served as pastor when I was in seminary. Ruby Fern had a debilitating illness. When I went back to the church several years ago, I walked out to the church cemetery and saw mother and daughter buried next to each other. When I was their pastor, I knew of their simple, unadulterated faith. I have never met anyone else who had more of a child-like faith in the power of God than Ruby and Ruby Fern. They walked simply and humbly with God. Obviously, Ruby used to pray for her daughter to be healed. The whole church prayed for wholeness in the physical brokenness of this young woman's life. But both of these women understood something about faith that spoke to the rest of us. Sometimes God may change the circumstances. Sometimes God may give us the strength to endure. Both are miracles of grace. Both take faith.

The Gate and the Pool

The "Sheep Gate" mentioned in this episode from the life of Jesus was an entrance through the city walls in Jerusalem (5:2). Located in the northeastern corner of the wall, the gate served as the entrance point for sheep that were to be sacrificed in the temple worship.

The pool of Bethesda was located near the sheep gate. The pool served as a popular gathering place. Apparently because of the legend of healings associated with it (5:7), the pool at Bethesda was a place where people who sought healing would gather.

A second aspect of this story is that the man who was healed didn't show that much faith. He did get up when Jesus told him to pick up his mat and walk. However, later in the day when the religious authorities asked who had healed him on the Sabbath, he told them he didn't have any idea. The man did not know who Jesus of Nazareth was (5:13). Apparently he was so delighted to be on his feet that he raced down the road without stopping to ask, *By the way, I'd like to know who you are so when people ask who healed me, I can tell them.*

> While our faith is important, that faith is built on the secure foundation of God's grace.

What we have in this miracle is not so much a story about human faith but an account of the divine Jesus who possesses the power to change lives. While our faith is important, that faith is built on the secure foundation of God's grace. The power of God's grace is not limited by our faith or doubt.

By the pool of Bethesda, Jesus made his case that he is indeed God. This sign points not to the man who was healed but to Jesus who heals each of us in different ways.

A Strange Conflict (5:9b–24)

You would think that everyone would be excited about a miracle. A man had not walked in thirty-eight years. With one command from Jesus, he was on his feet. Some of the religious authorities had a problem, however. It's the Sabbath, and one of the Jewish laws was that nobody was permitted to carry a mat on the Sabbath (5:10).

Wayne Oates, one of the pioneers of the pastoral care movement and longtime professor at The Southern Baptist Theological Seminary and the University of Louisville School of Medicine, used to talk about "sick religion." The response of the authorities to the healed man carrying his mat is a classic example of sick, myopic religion. Shouldn't religion see the big picture? Here is the power of God at work. The man probably didn't even know the law about not carrying your mat on the Sabbath. He hadn't been able to carry *anything* for almost four decades, no matter what day it was! But for the religious authorities, the mat was the issue.

When these authorities finally met Jesus, the situation got even more complicated. The Gospel of John says they started persecuting Jesus because he had healed on the Sabbath (5:16). Jesus answered, "My Father is still working, and I also am working" (5:17). If Jesus intended to quiet the controversy, that was not a good answer. The authorities were furious (5:18). What Jesus had done was to equate himself with God.

To try to understand the fury of the Jewish authorities, we have to remember how important monotheism and the various laws were to faithful Jews. Monotheism says there is only one God. One of the misunderstandings that some people have of the Christian faith is that they think Christians believe in three gods. Christians have always acknowledged the difficulty in expressing the doctrine of the Trinity. However, classical Christian doctrine has always been careful to affirm that there is one God who manifests himself in Father, Son, and Holy Spirit.

Some truths are beyond our human reason.

We can see the sadness of a religion that puts more emphasis on a mat than a man, but we have to understand, too, how important keeping the law was to the Jews. Dominated as they often were by greater military powers like the Roman Empire, the Jews saw obedience to the law of God as the way to maintain their identity as a people. What would happen if the religious authorities let some unknown, itinerant preacher tell people that a law should be broken? The Jews saw that as a slippery slope that would eventually lead to the abolition of their rigid system of laws and their identity as a people.

Such notions remind us that behind seemingly odd religious behaviors, there are reasons—odd reasons perhaps, but reasons nonetheless. Some experts believe that the primary driving force behind the resurgence of Islamic fundamentalism is the insecurity that unless every jot and tittle of the Koran is rigidly interpreted and tightly enforced, the Muslim identity will be lost to cultural accommodation. Anyone—Christians included—can fall prey to such reasoning. The tragic side of this idea is that people become fearful and defensive. In the process, all ability is lost to rejoice in the surprising grace of God.

A Strong Witness (5:31–40)

Apparently Jesus intended for his words about his divine nature to be heard by the authorities. In verses 31–40 all conversation stopped. This dialogue was over. Figuratively speaking, Jesus stepped up to the podium to deliver the sermon or soliloquy. This is the summation of Jesus, who was

The Law

Torah is the Hebrew word for *law*. *Torah* also refers to the Pentateuch, the first five books of the Hebrew Bible.

In New Testament times, the law was more than a section of Scripture; it was central to Judaism. To observe the law was equivalent to doing the will of God. Pious Jews believed that the basic laws of what we call the Old Testament needed elaboration and interpretation. This elaboration and interpretation took the form of the oral laws. The oral laws expanded what the law commanded about keeping the Sabbath holy by stating in detail what could not be done. The oral law is thus the source of the notion that carrying a mat on the Sabbath is unacceptable work.

defending his identity. Jesus called on witnesses who have testified that he is the *logos* or divine Word from God.

The first witness is John the Baptist. Jesus called John a "burning and shining lamp" (5:35). Jesus was careful to say that the testimony of another human being cannot confirm that Jesus is God, but Jesus shared this word about John because for a while people listened to what John said. Besides, Jesus will call any witness to the stand who will help people understand he has come to bring people into a new, vibrant relationship with God.

The second witness, however, is far more impressive. Jesus indicated that his works are part of his Father's plan (5:36).

Moreover, in verse 37, Jesus stated that "the Father . . . has himself testified on my behalf." Jesus further said that the Scriptures, the Old Testament, if used carefully and openly would point to himself as the Messiah (5:39, 45). The Father testifies through the Scriptures.

I was interim pastor of a church where laypeople shared their thoughts on the seven last sayings of Jesus. One young woman was especially articulate and passionate. She cited a writer who, according to this woman, had given overwhelming proof from the Old Testament that Jesus was the Messiah. The woman's point was, *How can anybody not see beyond a shadow of doubt that Jesus is who he says he was?* As she spoke, I thought of a very bright, young Jewish man I know who doesn't see the Old Testament that way. Recognizing the truth about Jesus still calls for our faith.

I believe in God although I have never seen God.

60

What About Us?

In this Scripture passage in John 5, Jesus was making a case for his identity. Those who heard Jesus talk about these witnesses to his identity were being challenged to decide. So are we. Ultimately, though, we accept or reject that case based on our interpretation of Scripture and our faith that Jesus is God.

> *Those who heard Jesus talk about these witnesses to his identity were being challenged to decide. So are we.*

Faith is different from taking something into the laboratory and proving it by the scientific method. Faith is using our best reasoning but knowing that reason is not the only road to truth. Some truths are beyond our human reason.

I believe in God although I have never seen God. I believe that Jesus is the Son of God. Can I prove this belief beyond everybody's doubt? No. Do I believe it with all my mind, heart, and soul? Yes! What about you?

QUESTIONS

1. Why do so many people believe that miracles have to be dramatic, extraordinary events? What is a miracle?

2. Why do you think Jesus asked the man (5:6), "Do you want to be made well?"

3. The Pharisees were more concerned about carrying a mat on the Sabbath than about a person's healing. When do we—as individuals, as a church, as a denomination—become distracted from Jesus' mission of changing people's lives and bringing them into relationship with God?

4. Why do you believe that Jesus is the Son of God?

The Growing Conflict

Popularity can be fleeting. Sam Houston, hero of the Battle of San Jacinto and first president of the Republic of Texas, had it and then lost it. Houston served his adopted state of Texas as one of its first United States Senators during a time when the nation simmered with unrest. Northern and southern states battled over laws that would limit slavery. Sectionalism grew rapidly in the decade before the Civil War.

Houston, who (by the way) was a Baptist, believed in the nation. He voiced repeatedly and regularly his conviction that the nation should remain united and the problems addressed from within as a united nation. Other Texans violently disagreed. Some called for him to resign as senator. Houston was defeated in a run for governor of Texas in 1857, but he staged an upset comeback with a victory in 1859. He resigned as governor in 1861, refusing to take an oath of allegiance to the Confederacy.[1]

Houston maintained his integrity while proclaiming an unpopular message. Conflict in the later years of his life diminished his earlier popularity.

In a far more significant way, Jesus was another whose popularity reached a peak and waned. His fame and prestige grew rapidly during the first year of his public ministry. Turning water into wine and healing a lame man captured the attention of the common people. They flocked to him while Jewish leaders were beginning to recognize the threat he posed to them. His popularity peaked on a Galilean hillside where he fed more than 5,000 who gathered to hear him teach and then attempted to make him king.

In this two-session unit, we will see how Jesus' acclaim with the crowds dwindled as many of his followers deserted him. Lesson six reveals how they followed him as long as he fed them. When they realized that he expected them to commit themselves to him, their devotion disappeared. When he began to speak of eating his flesh and drinking his blood, they deserted him (John 6:53–66). They could accept him as a wonder-worker, but not as the "Holy One of God" (6:69, NASB).[2]

We will see in lesson seven that opposition from the Jewish leaders increased. The intensity of their hostility boiled over when Jesus healed a blind man on the Sabbath. Jesus chose this time to declare that he was the "Light of the world" (8:12), the "door of the sheep" (10:7), and the "good shepherd" (10:10). He offered spiritual insight to those who would believe.

UNIT TWO, THE GROWING CONFLICT

Lesson 6   To Whom Shall We Go?   John 6:41–58, 66–69
Lesson 7   The Good Shepherd
            and Human Blindness   John 9:1–7; 9:39—10:19

NOTES

1. See John F. Kennedy, *Profiles in Courage*, Memorial Edition, Perennial Library (New York: Harper and Row, 1964); Marquis James, *The Raven: A Biography of Sam Houston* (Austin: University of Texas Press, reprinted from the 1929 Bobbs Merrill edition), 388–412; *The Handbook of Texas Online*, www.tsha.utexas.edu/handbook/online/
2. Unless otherwise indicated, all Scripture quotations in Unit Two are from the New American Standard Bible®, Copyright © The Lockman Foundation 1960, 1962, 1963, 1968, 1971, 1972, 1973, 1975, 1977, 1995. Used by permission.

Focal Text

John 6:41–58, 66–69

Background

John 6—8

Main Idea

Jesus calls us so to commit ourselves to him that we base every aspect of our lives on him.

Question to Explore

Do you believe in Jesus because of what he does for you or because of who he is?

Study Aim

To state the significance for my life of Jesus as the bread of life and evaluate the extent of my commitment to him

Study and Action Emphases

- Affirm the Bible as our authoritative guide for life and ministry
- Share the gospel with all people
- Develop a growing, vibrant faith

LESSON SIX

To Whom Shall We Go?

Quick Read

Jesus' feeding of the multitude with five loaves and two fish provided Jesus the opportunity to declare that in him and him alone people could find eternal life.

65

In a short story called "The Son from America," Polish-born writer Isaac Singer tells the story of the son who became rich during a forty-year stay in the United States. The son returned to Europe to visit his father. The village had remained the same. He asked his father what he had done with the money orders that the son had sent every year. The father showed him an old boot in which he had kept the money. The son asked why the father had never spent the money.

The old man replied that he had everything he needed. The son probed. The answer was the same; his father lacked nothing. The son wandered around the village. As he watched the people, he indeed realized that they needed nothing. They had everything. Material needs were not foremost in the minds of the villagers.

The villagers differed from those who ate the bread when Jesus fed the multitude in John 6. They pursued him for another meal. They desired the material things he could offer but balked when he offered them something greater—eternal life.

Some people follow Jesus for what he gives to them. Others follow because of who he is. Today's lesson will help us to see that Jesus is the One whom we can trust with our whole existence and future.

Christ, the Bread of Life (6:41–51)

Chapter 6 recounts the miracle of Jesus' feeding the multitude with five loaves and two fish, followed by a lengthy conversation between Jesus and the people. The heart of this discourse is his declaration, "I am the bread of life" (6:35, 48). This declaration draws its inspiration from the miracle. The events and discussion that followed amplified what he meant by the statement.

Jesus had crossed the Sea of Galilee (Tiberias) to be with his disciples. The crowds followed him, hoping he would continue to heal the sick. It was spring and near the time for the Passover feast. Jesus asked Philip where they could find food for the multitude (6:5). Philip did not have an answer. Andrew, though, found a boy who had five loaves and two fish. Jesus instructed the people to sit and gave thanks. He then began to break the bread and distribute it to the crowd. Everyone in attendance ate until full. The disciples gathered twelve baskets of leftovers.

The people reacted to the miracle by mounting a campaign to make Jesus their king. Their effort was rooted in Jewish tradition. God had

John 6:41–58, 66–69

41Therefore the Jews were grumbling about Him, because He said, "I am the bread that came down out of heaven." 42They were saying, "Is not this Jesus, the son of Joseph, whose father and mother we know? How does He now say, 'I have come down out of heaven'?" 43Jesus answered and said to them, "Do not grumble among yourselves. 44"No one can come to Me unless the Father who sent Me draws him; and I will raise him up on the last day. 45"It is written in the prophets, 'AND THEY SHALL ALL BE TAUGHT OF GOD.' Everyone who has heard and learned from the Father, comes to Me. 46"Not that anyone has seen the Father, except the One who is from God; He has seen the Father. 47"Truly, truly, I say to you, he who believes has eternal life. 48"I am the bread of life. 49"Your fathers ate the manna in the wilderness, and they died. 50"This is the bread which comes down out of heaven, so that one may eat of it and not die. 51"I am the living bread that came down out of heaven; if anyone eats of this bread, he will live forever; and the bread also which I will give for the life of the world is My flesh."

52Then the Jews began to argue with one another, saying, "How can this man give us His flesh to eat?" 53So Jesus said to them, "Truly, truly, I say to you, unless you eat the flesh of the Son of Man and drink His blood, you have no life in yourselves. 54"He who eats My flesh and drinks My blood has eternal life, and I will raise him up on the last day. 55"For My flesh is true food, and My blood is true drink. 56"He who eats My flesh and drinks My blood abides in Me, and I in him. 57"As the living Father sent Me, and I live because of the Father, so he who eats Me, he also will live because of Me. 58"This is the bread which came down out of heaven; not as the fathers ate and died; he who eats this bread will live forever."

• •

66As a result of this many of His disciples withdrew and were not walking with Him anymore. 67So Jesus said to the twelve, "You do not want to go away also, do you?" 68Simon Peter answered Him, "Lord, to whom shall we go? You have words of eternal life. 69"We have believed and have come to know that You are the Holy One of God."

stopped sending manna to the Hebrews when they celebrated their first Passover in the Promised Land (Joshua 4:11–12). The people had long believed that the Messiah would again bring bread from heaven. Passover was on the minds of the people when Jesus multiplied the loaves. The miracles persuaded them that this bread-maker might be their Messiah. Jesus withdrew to the mountain to prevent them from crowning him Messiah (John 6:15).

The disciples finally returned across the sea to Capernaum without Jesus. When a storm arose during the night, Jesus came to them, walking on the water. The crowd located them the next day in Capernaum and asked Jesus how he got there. He curtly answered that what they really wanted was not his itinerary but more food.

> . . . Jesus is the One whom we can trust with our whole existence and future.

Jesus had provided them one meal of bread and fish. Now they wanted breakfast. He told them that all physical bread would perish, but the bread that he could supply would fill them forever (6:27, 35). They were still thinking in material terms when they asked for this bread. How wonderful it would be never to hunger again.

The crowd's conversation with Jesus paralleled his earlier conversation with the Samaritan woman (John 4). He and the woman began talking about water from the well. Jesus introduced the concept of living water, which the woman believed would satisfy her physical thirst. He then guided her to understand that the living water he would provide was eternal life.

The focal passage opens with the Jews grumbling about Jesus' claim to be the "bread that came down from heaven" (6:41). John normally used the term "Jews" for Jewish leaders or those who opposed Jesus. Many of the "Jews" were Pharisees or high-ranking members of the Sanhedrin. Those who grumbled here may have been leaders of the synagogue in Capernaum since that was the site for the encounter.

> Jesus is the bread through which a person comes to the Father and to life.

Chapter 6, and perhaps even this verse (6:41), marks a turning point for Jesus in John's Gospel. He had been extremely popular before these events and the subsequent conversation. Sporadic opposition had appeared before, but hereafter hostility would escalate. "Grumbling" suggests the murmuring that runs through a crowd when they become angry or hostile.

The grumbling of the Capernaum Jews likely alludes to the grumbling of the Hebrews as they wandered in the wilderness (Exodus 15:24; 16:2; Numbers 11:4–6). Those Jews grumbled against Moses directly and against God indirectly when they did not have enough water or wanted meat to eat. To grumble against Jesus and his claims amounted to rejection of Jesus himself.

These murmuring Jews remembered the stories about the wilderness wandering and the impressive wonders Moses performed there. They expected the Messianic deliverer to perform the same kind of miracles. The people wanted to crown Jesus as king when their stomachs were full beside the sea, but their leaders were not impressed by Jesus' miracles. They might have been able to accept Jesus' works, but they could not accept his claim to be divine.

Jesus described himself as the bread of life and the "bread that came down out of heaven" (John 6:51; see also 6:33, 38, 41, 42, 50, 51, 58). Because Jesus "came down" from heaven, those who sought eternal life needed to "come to him" in belief (see 6:37–40).

One reason the crowd challenged Jesus' claim was that they knew his family and lineage. The Jews expected mystery and secrecy to surround the origin of the Messiah. Verse 42 states that the crowds knew Jesus' family. They knew, or at least knew of, his parents. Because Jesus had lived for years as one of them, they could not accept his current claim that he was sent from heaven.

Jesus replied to their charges and told them to stop grumbling. He ignored their literal understanding of his statements and redirected their thoughts to God's initiative in providing salvation. Only those whom the Father drew to Christ could come to him and receive him. We must balance this statement with Jesus' words in John 3:16: "For God so loved the world, that He gave His only begotten Son, that *whoever* believes in Him shall not perish, but have eternal life" (italics by the writer for emphasis). Jesus quoted from either Isaiah 54:13 or Jeremiah 31:34 to indicate that those who learned from the Father would come to Christ as the one through whom they would receive access to God.

> *Christ came to reveal the character and personality of God.*

In John 6:46, which reminds us of John 1:18, Jesus clarified that the only person to have seen the Father was the one sent by the Father. Jesus clearly referred to himself as the only one who could show people what God was truly like. Christ came to reveal the character and personality of God.

In verses 47–51 Jesus explained what he meant when he claimed to be the bread of life. Eternal life comes not from physical bread but from believing in Jesus. The tense of "believes" in 6:47 denotes a life that is characterized by belief. The word thus refers to a state of faith in Jesus that allows a person to receive eternal life. This verse shows what Jesus meant when he said one needed to eat of the bread and the flesh. Jesus meant that the person was to believe and trust him.

Jesus reaffirmed in verse 48 that he is the bread of life. The statement's briefness gives it an emphasis that would impress the hearers. Jesus is the bread through which a person comes to the Father and to life.

Jesus reminded the Jews that their fathers had eaten manna and died anyway (6:49). The manna that Moses provided could not effect in them eternal life, or even everlasting physical life. The manna that came from heaven could not prevent death, but the person who partook of the bread of the life of Jesus would not die. Jesus used "die" in two ways. In verse 49 he meant physical death. In verse 50 he meant spiritual death. The tense of the word translated "eat" suggests a one-time action by which a person receives Christ.

Genuine spiritual sustenance comes through incorporating Christ into our lives by faith.

Jesus summed up in verse 51 what he had been saying. The key to life is to eat of the bread that came down from heaven, Jesus. Our Lord added that the bread to which he referred was his flesh. The mention of flesh points to his sacrificial death. He introduced here the idea that his death would be voluntary for the whole world.

Appropriating Jesus as the Bread of Life (6:52–58)

The Jewish authorities argued among themselves over Jesus' statements. Perhaps some of them understood what Jesus implied and were willing to accept him. Others were not. They could not agree on how Jesus could give them his flesh to eat. In the discourses in John's Gospel, Jesus would often make a puzzling statement and then explain it when people raised objections to it. Examples include "unless one is born again he cannot see the kingdom of God" (3:3) and "destroy this temple, and in three days I will raise it up" (2:19). The authorities knew that Jesus was not speaking about cannibalism, but they still found the words offensive. They wondered what they might mean.

While the authorities were squabbling over what eating flesh meant, Jesus added that they needed to drink his blood also. Without doing this,

Miracles in John's Gospel

Jesus performed many miracles during his public ministry. Despite the large number in Matthew, Mark, and Luke, the Gospel of John records but seven. The Gospel of John employs this small number to emphasize more than simply the power of God at work in Christ. It uses them to reveal special aspects of Jesus' personality or character, generally referring to them as "signs" or "works." Note these miracles in the Gospel of John and their meaning:

(1) When Jesus turned water into wine, he pointed to himself as the one who fulfilled the Jewish heritage but carried it to a higher level (2:1–11).

(2) When Jesus healed the royal official's son, he pointed to his power to provide eternal life (4:46–54).

(3) When Jesus healed the invalid at the pool of Bethesda, he asserted that he was working the works of the Father (5:1–15).

(4) When Jesus fed the 5,000, he claimed that he was the bread of life, the one who provides life from heaven (6:1–14, 25–69).

(5) When Jesus walked on the water, he claimed to be the divine "I am" (6:16–21; see Exodus 3:13–16).

(6) When Jesus restored sight to the man born blind, he declared that he was the light to the world, the one who bestows spiritual insight (9:1–41).

(7) When Jesus raised Lazarus, he illustrated his role as the resurrection and the life (11:1–44).

they would have no life. The Mosaic law prohibited the drinking of any blood (Leviticus 3:17). Thus, the leaders found these words highly repulsive. The reference to eating flesh and drinking blood means taking Christ into our innermost being. Both flesh and blood would remind the people about their sacrificial practices. Both call attention to death. Jesus was asserting that life came not through some new teaching or law but through his life and death. Those who accept Christ's sacrificial death by faith will receive life. He will raise them up on the last day.

Genuine spiritual sustenance comes through incorporating Christ into our lives by faith. Jesus described what he meant when he said that the one who would eat his flesh and drink his blood would abide continuously in him.

Jesus lived because of his relationship to the Father who had sent him. His work was the Father's work (John 10:37–38). Jesus promised to impart this life to those who would trust and receive him.

The Jewish leaders considered Moses to be great. He had delivered the Hebrews from Egyptian slavery, guided them through the wilderness, and taught them God's commandments for living. He had provided manna for them during their journeys, but their fathers still died. Those who would accept Christ's death would live forever, even if they died physically.

Peter's Great Confession (6:66–69)

Many of Jesus' disciples understood what he said and left him. They no longer walked with him. This suggests that they had both physically and spiritually returned to their previous lives. Jesus had made it plain that following him as a disciple would be difficult.

The Gospel of John distinguishes between the twelve and the larger crowd of disciples who abandoned Jesus. This is the first time "the twelve" is mentioned in John (6:67). Jesus asked them whether they too were going to return to their old lives. We could paraphrase his question in 6:67, *You are not going to leave, too, are you?* The form of the question expects a negative answer. Jesus expected the twelve to remain.

The source for eternal life is Jesus.

As was often the case, Peter responded and spoke for all the apostles. He stated that they could not go to anyone else because he alone had the words that brought life. Peter's statement parallels his confession in the other gospels (Matthew 16:16; Mark 8:29; Luke 9:20). The title "Lord" in John 6:68 expresses the full concept of deity. Peter's confession

Jesus' "I Am" statements

Jesus made seven emphatic "I am" statements in John's Gospel. Each of these highlights some facet of Jesus' ministry and work. These are: (1) the bread of life (6:35); (2) "the Light of the world" (8:12); (3) "the door of the sheep" (10:7); (4) "the good shepherd" (10:11); (5) "the resurrection and the life" (11:25); (6) "the way, the truth, and the life" (14:6); and (7) "the true vine" (15:1).

The words "I am" suggest a claim of divinity. When God identified himself to Moses at the burning bush he named himself as "I AM" (Exodus 3:14). Jesus also used the term in John 8:58, where the people certainly understood it as a claim to be divine. (The term can also be seen in the Greek of other verses, such as John 6:20; 8:28; 18:5–8.)

in John 6:68–69 provides a clear interpretation of what Jesus meant by eating his flesh and drinking his blood.

Peter's use of the pronoun "we" in 6:69 emphasized the twelve in contrast to those who deserted Jesus. The verbs "have believed" and "have come to know" show a fixed and settled condition. The twelve had made a conscious decision with lasting consequences. In the Greek of 6:69, Peter also emphasized the word "you" in referring to Jesus. Jesus alone was the "Holy One of God." This title, used rarely for Jesus in the New Testament, portrays Jesus' exalted status. It seems to be equivalent to Messiah or Anointed One. To call Jesus "holy" affirms that he belongs to God. The word restates the idea that Jesus came from the Father and accomplished the Father's will.

> *Jesus, the Bread of Life, is the basic source of life for any of us.*

Implications for Us

When I visit my favorite cafeteria, I'm glad they put the desserts last in line. As it is, the choices that are available can be overwhelming. If I'm not careful, I'll pass by the food that offers the best nourishment and head for that which doesn't.

The possibilities for direction and purpose in life are likewise overwhelming. We can easily choose from those options that provide no substance or permanence. Jesus, the Bread of Life, is the basic source of life for any of us. The source for eternal life is Jesus. We receive that life when we eat the Bread, giving ourselves without reservation to Jesus.

QUESTIONS

1. What are some ways in which we follow Jesus for what he does for us rather than for who he is?

2. What are some demands Jesus makes that challenge our commitment to follow him?

3. What are some other teachings of Jesus that you find hard to accept?

4. How do we withdraw from Jesus when following him becomes difficult?

5. How does the Father draw us to Christ?

6. How can you harmonize the concepts that "whoever believes" (John 3:16) will have eternal life with the statement, "No one can come to Me unless the Father who sent Me draws him" (6:44)?

7. What had Peter seen in Christ that prompted his great confession? What have you seen that would prompt you to make the same confession?

Focal Text

John 9:1–7; 9:39—10:19

Background

John 9—10

Main Idea

Jesus provides abundant life to all who will let him open their eyes.

Question to Explore

We couldn't be blind, could we?

Study Aim

To identify ways in which I could be spiritually blind

Study and Action Emphases

- Affirm the Bible as our authoritative guide for life and ministry
- Share the gospel with all people
- Develop a growing, vibrant faith

LESSON SEVEN

The Good Shepherd and Human Blindness

Quick Read

Jesus healed a blind man and used the sign to illustrate and proclaim that he can provide abundant life to those whose spiritual eyes are open to him.

Two men, one old and one young, shared the platform before a large audience. According to the story, each was to recite Psalm 23. The young man was highly trained in speech and drama. When he finished, the crowd clapped and cheered, asking for an encore. Then the old man stood before the crowd and spoke in a feeble voice: "The Lord is my Shepherd . . . ." When he finished, a hush filled the room. Folks were seen praying.

The young man stood again and explained, "Do you know the difference between my presentation of the Twenty-third Psalm and my friend's? I know the psalm, but he knows the Shepherd."

Jesus declared that those with spiritual insight know Jesus as the Son of God. Jesus knows them as a shepherd knows his flock.

Jesus Heals a Blind Man (9:1–7)

Jesus continued to minister in Jerusalem despite increasing hostility from the Jewish authorities (John 7:1; 8:59). One Sabbath Jesus and the disciples encountered a man who had been blind from birth.

The disciples' first words after seeing the man concerned blame. Whose fault was it that he was blind? Was his blindness caused by his parents' sin or his own? The belief that sin directly caused major illnesses persisted in Jesus' day despite the teachings of the Book of Job. Jews of that time often believed that God would visit the punishment of parents and grandparents down to the third and fourth generations (Exodus 34:7), in spite of the teachings of Ezekiel 18. Some rabbis even taught that an infant might sin in the womb.

Jesus refused to become trapped in the disciples' discussion. His reply neatly sidestepped the dilemma created by their question. Neither this man nor his parents should be blamed. Jesus stated that he would now minister to the man and the works of God would be demonstrated in the miracle. Jesus chose ministry over debate.

The man needed help. Jesus refused to ignore his plight. His answer to their question used the plural "we" to refer to those who helped and "me" to himself, the One whom God had sent (John 9:4). By phrasing the response in this way, Jesus indicated that his followers shared his responsibility to minister. Jesus expected his disciples to minister as he ministered, both then and now.

Jesus recognized that he would not always have the opportunity to help others. He could act only in the present, which he described as "day" (9:4).

John 9:1–7, 39–41

[1]As He passed by, He saw a man blind from birth. [2]And His disciples asked Him, "Rabbi, who sinned, this man or his parents, that he would be born blind?" [3]Jesus answered, "It was neither that this man sinned, nor his parents; but it was so that the works of God might be displayed in him. [4]"We must work the works of Him who sent Me as long as it is day; night is coming when no one can work. [5]"While I am in the world, I am the Light of the world." [6]When He had said this, He spat on the ground, and made clay of the spittle, and applied the clay to his eyes, [7]and said to him, "Go, wash in the pool of Siloam" (which is translated, Sent). So he went away and washed, and came back seeing.

· ·

[39]And Jesus said, "For judgment I came into this world, so that those who do not see may see, and that those who see may become blind." [40]Those of the Pharisees who were with Him heard these things and said to Him, "We are not blind too, are we?" [41]Jesus said to them, "If you were blind, you would have no sin; but since you say, 'We see,' your sin remains.

John 10:1–19

[1]"Truly, truly, I say to you, he who does not enter by the door into the fold of the sheep, but climbs up some other way, he is a thief and a robber. [2]"But he who enters by the door is a shepherd of the sheep. [3]"To him the doorkeeper opens, and the sheep hear his voice, and he calls his own sheep by name and leads them out. [4]"When he puts forth all his own, he goes ahead of them, and the sheep follow him because they know his voice. [5]"A stranger they simply will not follow, but will flee from him, because they do not know the voice of strangers." [6]This figure of speech Jesus spoke to them, but they did not understand what those things were which He had been saying to them.

[7]So Jesus said to them again, "Truly, truly, I say to you, I am the door of the sheep. [8]"All who came before Me are thieves and robbers, but the sheep did not hear them. [9]"I am the door; if anyone enters through Me, he will be saved, and will go in and out and find pasture. [10]"The thief comes only to steal and kill and destroy; I came that they may have life, and have it abundantly.

[11]"I am the good shepherd; the good shepherd lays down His life for the sheep. [12]"He who is a hired hand, and not a shepherd, who is not the

owner of the sheep, sees the wolf coming, and leaves the sheep and flees, and the wolf snatches them and scatters them. ¹³"He flees because he is a hired hand and is not concerned about the sheep. ¹⁴"I am the good shepherd, and I know My own and My own know Me, ¹⁵even as the Father knows Me and I know the Father; and I lay down My life for the sheep. ¹⁶"I have other sheep, which are not of this fold; I must bring them also, and they will hear My voice; and they will become one flock *with* one shepherd. ¹⁷"For this reason the Father loves Me, because I lay down My life so that I may take it again. ¹⁸"No one has taken it away from Me, but I lay it down on My own initiative. I have authority to lay it down, and I have authority to take it up again. This commandment I received from My Father."

¹⁹A division occurred again among the Jews because of these words.

He, the light of the world, would soon depart it, and the world would be without him. The "night" would be the time after he left. Jesus' reference to the short time in which he had to serve may have reflected the authorities' threat to stone him. Jesus reminded the disciples that the works he was doing were determined by the One who sent him.

Jesus had set the stage for the healing of the blind man, the sixth miraculous sign recorded in John (see article, "Miracles in John's Gospel," in lesson six). Why Jesus chose to spit and make clay to apply to the man's eyes is not known (9:6). We do know that saliva was thought by many in the ancient world to have curative power.

Jesus declared that those with spiritual insight know Jesus as the Son of God.

Jesus smeared the mud paste on the blind man's eyes and instructed him to go to the pool of Siloam to wash it off. Jesus offered no promise that the man would be healed when he washed off the clay, although the man's action in going to the pool leads us to believe that he thought he would be. The blind man obeyed Jesus and came back with restored sight.

Some scholars see in the use of clay a reference to Genesis 2:7: "Then the Lord God formed man of dust from the ground, and breathed into his nostrils the breath of life; and man became a living being." Such a reference would suggest we are to consider Jesus' act to be a new work of creation.

The pool received its name, "Siloam" (meaning "Sent"), because it collected water inside the city walls. The water had been channeled through rock from the Gihon Spring in the Kidron Valley. Perhaps John understood the reference to "Siloam" symbolically as well as literally. He frequently stressed that the Father had *sent* Jesus (see, for example, John 4:34; 5:24; 6:44). The One "sent" from God healed the blind man.

A great debate and controversy followed (9:13–34). Some people wondered whether this was the same man who had been blind. The Pharisees involved themselves when they realized he was the same man and that Jesus had healed him on the Sabbath. They grilled the man about the identity of the One who had healed him. All that the man could report was that he could see. His parents refused to answer questions because they feared retaliation by the Jewish leaders.

The authorities again interrogated the man. They challenged his testimony, insisting that he glorify God instead of the one who had healed him. They maintained that only God could perform this kind of miracle and that anyone who healed on the Sabbath could not be from God. The man saw the absurdity of their reasoning. He started from another place. He

Jesus chose ministry over debate.

pointed out that he had been blind and Jesus had healed him. If only God could restore sight, then Jesus must be from God. In response, the Pharisees threw the man out from their presence.

Jesus knew what was happening to the man and found him after the Pharisees had thrown him out (9:35–38). He asked the man whether he believed in the Son of Man. When the man wanted to know more and indicated his desire to see him, Jesus identified himself as the Son of Man. Then the man worshiped Jesus.

The Need for Spiritual Vision (9:39–41)

Jesus' words in verse 39 do not seem necessarily addressed to the blind man. Others, including the Pharisees, may have overheard the conversation with the blind man. Jesus announced that he came into the world "for judgment" (9:39). How can we reconcile this statement with those verses where Jesus stated that he did not come to judge (3:17; 12:47)? It helps to distinguish between judgment as division and condemnation. Jesus did not come to condemn or punish. He came to show the path to abundant life. When confronted with his message and teaching, people judge themselves as they decide to follow or reject Jesus.

The Son came so the blind might see and those who could see might become blind. "Those who do not see" are those who have no spiritual vision but understand their need. "Those who see" are those who mistakenly believe that they have spiritual vision. Some Pharisees who had overheard Jesus' statements asked him whether he thought they were spiritually blind. The form of their question shows their belief that they were not spiritually blind.

> So enamored were they with themselves and their system, they could not fathom that they had any spiritual need.

Jesus' reply surely shocked them. Jesus asserted that they would have been better off had they been spiritually blind (9:41). So enamored were they with themselves and their system, they could not fathom that they had any spiritual need. Jesus could have helped them had they recognized their need. Because they refused to acknowledge their condition, they remained in sin and self-delusion.

The Parable of the Sheepfold (10:1–6)

Several factors suggest that this parable continues the flow from the previous chapter. (1) The words translated "very truly" never introduce something new. They always reinforce something that has been previously introduced. (2) The reference in 10:19–21 to the healing of the blind man seems to bracket these verses to that incident. (3) The Jewish leaders had rejected the man and cast him out of the synagogue. Jesus told the story to illustrate how unfaithful they had been. They were sapping the life out of people by their legalism. They failed to direct people to the abundant life God desired for them.

The "figure of speech" (10:6) contains two significant images: (1) the door of the "fold" or pen; and (2) the shepherd. Jesus described those who enter the pen by any way except the door as thieves and robbers. A sheep "fold" or pen was usually a stone structure, perhaps mud-brick, that had only one opening through which the sheep entered. The word "thief" (10:1) implies entering by trickery. "Robber" (10:1) suggests violence. The shepherd would enter through the door. Those who wished to harm the sheep would enter in other ways.

A pen frequently held the flocks of several shepherds. Each shepherd would come to the enclosure in the morning and call to his sheep. His

"So That"

The phrase "so that" in John 9:3 has caused considerable dialogue among Bible students. Some suggest that the words imply purpose, which is the normal usage in the Greek. Thus, the purpose of the man's blindness was that Jesus could perform a miracle to reveal the power and glory of God.

Some people struggle with an interpretation that views God as deliberately causing a person to be born blind. That belief does not harmonize with how they sense God working. Some commentators have dealt with this issue by connecting the purpose clause with the phrase that follows rather than with the one that goes before. We should recall that the original Greek had little, if any, punctuation. In most cases, the punctuation is straightforward, but not always. This may be one of those cases in which the punctuation must be determined by interpretation. Thus the meaning could be as follows: *In order for God's power to be demonstrated, we are going to do God's works in the present moment.*

Another option is that the purpose was the healing and not the blindness. Still another possibility is that the phrase expresses result and not purpose. The Greek words can be understood in this way, thus suggesting that the blindness was not caused by God but was rather simply associated with the man's birth.

---

sheep recognized his unique call and followed him to pasture. They followed because they recognized him. They would flee from those who imitated the call. Note that Jesus spoke this "figure of speech" because the people did not understand what he was trying to teach them (10:6).

Jesus: "The Door" (10:7–10)

In verses 6–18, Jesus interpreted the figure of speech. The failure of the Jews to understand was not an intellectual problem but a spiritual one. They refused to believe in the identity of Jesus.

Jesus concentrated on the first image of the parable by declaring, "I am the door of the sheep" (10:7). He amplified the statement in two ways. First, he restated that those who enter through any way but the door are thieves and robbers. The sheep would not hear the voices of strangers. Second, Jesus is the door through which the sheep enter the sheepfold. The shepherd regulated the entrance of the sheep through the one door. Jesus, not the Jewish leaders, provided

Jesus indicated that his followers shared his responsibility to minister.

access to life. "Through me" is in an emphatic position in the Greek (10:9). No other door provides an entrance to eternal life. Those who seek to find life in Jesus will find it. Jesus' sheep will find safety and security in him as they "go in and out" (10:9).

Jesus' characterization of "all who came before Me" as "thieves and robbers" creates some interpretive difficulty (10:8). It is difficult to see how he could have meant faithful leaders of the Old Testament. The best understanding is that "thieves and robbers" refers to the Pharisees and other Jewish leaders of the previous chapter. Thieves had only evil intent in mind, seeking to destroy and kill the sheep. On the other hand, Jesus came that people might have abundant life.

Jesus came that people might have abundant life.

The word "I" in the expressions "I am the door" (10:7, 9) and "I came that they may have life" (10:10) is emphatic in the Greek. These expressions thus strongly contrast Jesus' work to that of the Jewish leaders. "Abundantly" means a surplus, an overflowing. Abundant life is one of grace, joy, and peace.

Jesus: "The Good Shepherd" (10:11–18)

Jesus summarized the second part of the figure of speech (10:1–5) in the words, "I am the good shepherd" (10:11). As Jesus drew two interpretations of "I am the gate," he also drew two conclusions from this summary statement. One is that the good shepherd would die willingly for his sheep (10:11–13, 15b–18). The other is that the good shepherd knew his sheep intimately (10:14–15a).

Consider first the good shepherd's intimate knowledge of the sheep. The verb "know" (10:14) means more than recognizing facts. It implies trust and intimacy. For God to know his flock is for God to have a relationship with them. In return, God's flock, God's people, know and trust God. Jesus had said earlier that the sheep recognized the good shepherd's voice (10:3–5). Jesus reinforced the closeness of this relationship by comparing it to the intimacy between himself and the Father (10:15a).

Jesus' sheep will find safety and security in him . . . .

Jesus noted also that he had other sheep in his fold that he needed to join with the present flock. He distinguished between the enclosure ("fold") and the sheep ("flock," 10:16). These other sheep, outside the current pen, would join those already contained within. All would become part of his one flock.

Jesus seems to have been referring to the inclusion of Gentiles. The disciples may not have fully understood the implications of his words at that time, but they did by the time the Gospel of John was written. To bring others into the flock was not a wish but a compelling necessity ("must," 10:16). Paul wrote that Christ had broken down the wall that separated Jew and Gentile (Ephesians 2:11–21).

The other facet of the good shepherd was his willingness to lay down his life for his sheep (John 10:11, 15, 17–18). The image of laying down one's life appears also in 13:37–38; 15:13. The good shepherd's laying down his life "for the sheep" (10:11, 15) means for their benefit.

Jesus contrasted himself with the Jewish authorities when he said the shepherd would die for his sheep, but the hired hand would not. The worker would run instead of protecting the sheep. He would run simply because he was hired and not the owner. Jesus, the Good Shepherd, cared for the sheep because they belonged to him.

Jesus saw his death not as defeat but victory.

Jesus closed his explanation of the parable by stating that God loved him because he laid down his life for the sheep (see 10:17–18). What is meant is that Jesus' dying was God's will for his life. The Father loved him because he was dedicated to accomplishing the task for which he was sent. We can again see evidence of the intimacy between Father and Son.

Jesus chose to lay down his life so he might take it up again. Death is often linked to resurrection in John's Gospel. Jesus saw his death not as

Jesus' Healing of the Blind

Jesus used different means to express his healing power in restoring sight to the blind. He healed some by simply touching their eyes (Matthew 9:27–30). He spat on the eyes of a man in Bethsaida as he laid his hands on him. When the man replied that he could see only shadows moving, Jesus touched his eyes. The man could then see clearly (Mark 8:22–26). Jesus brought sight to Bartimaeus by stating that he could see (Mark 10:46–52).

By using different means to heal, Jesus was able to focus on the miracle and his power and not on how it was done. He was the source of the healing in each instance. Each healing was unique to the individual whose sight was restored.

defeat but victory. In his death and resurrection, Jesus would glorify his Father. Jesus emphasized the voluntary nature of his death (10:17–18). He had the authority to take up his life after he had laid it down. He was not a victim but a victor. He remained in control throughout it all.

The Bible states in other places that the Father raised Christ from the dead (see Acts 2:24; Romans 4:24; 1 Peter 1:21). Verse 18 states that the Son would take up his life. This does not imply a contradiction but an affirmation of the intimacy between Father and Son, for Father and Son are one (John 10:30).

A Division Among the People (10:19)

People chose sides after Jesus had finished speaking. Some Jews continued to reject him, but others believed, such as Nicodemus and Joseph of Arimathea. Jesus' work and message force people to decide to follow him or reject him.

Implications for Us

Jesus continues to divide people between disciples and nonbelievers. Those who choose not to believe in and trust Jesus remain spiritually blind and without eternal life. Those who have opened their eyes to the light he brought receive spiritual insight and eternal life.

QUESTIONS

1. What do you believe is the connection between sickness and sin?
2. How are we still spiritually blind? What have you discovered in today's text that will help dispel that spiritual darkness?
3. How have you missed seeing God working because it conflicted with your conceptions of how God works?
4. What "other sheep" (10:16) in your community can you identify that need to be included in your church?
5. What other "doors" do people substitute for Jesus?
6. How have you heard the Shepherd's voice in your life?

The Time Has Come

U N I T

T H R E E

A story from the siege of the Alamo in 1836 asserts that Colonel William Barret Travis took his sword and drew a line in the courtyard of the Alamo in San Antonio. He invited those who were willing to stay and defend it with him—and most likely to die doing so—to cross the line and join him. The volunteers understood that the time had come for them to stay or leave, to live or die for freedom. Through their sacrifice they allowed Sam Houston the time to ready his army for the decisive Texan victory at San Jacinto.

Although perhaps in not so dramatic a fashion, we all face those crisis times when we hold destiny in our hands. At such times, we recognize that the time has come to decide and to act.

When Jesus returned to Bethany to bring Lazarus to life again, he realized that his time had come. The ever-increasing antagonism of the Jewish authorities deepened even more when they heard that Lazarus was alive. They intensified their efforts to arrest Jesus as his reputation grew.

Jesus began to focus even more on the end of his life on earth. He used every opportunity to point to himself as the source of eternal life. The first session of this unit describes Jesus' raising of Lazarus and Jesus' claim that he was the resurrection and the life (John 11:1–54). The second lesson focuses on Jesus' offer of himself as Savior of the world in John 11:55—12:50.

Throughout these lessons, we will note that Jesus understood that his time had come and that he voluntarily laid down his life so that we might obtain eternal life. His offering of himself to secure our eternal life obligates us to accept or reject him.[1]

NOTES

1. Unless otherwise indicated, all Scripture quotations in Unit Three are from the New American Standard Bible®, Copyright © The Lockman Foundation 1960, 1962, 1963, 1968, 1971, 1972, 1973, 1975, 1977, 1995. Used by permission.

Focal Text

John 11:14–44, 47–53

Background

John 11:1–54

Main Idea

Jesus challenges us to respond to him as the One who offers and is the resurrection and the life.

Question to Explore

Do you believe this?

Study Aim

To respond to Jesus as the One who offers and is the resurrection and the life

Study and Action Emphases

- Affirm the Bible as our authoritative guide for life and ministry
- Share the gospel with all people
- Develop a growing, vibrant faith

LESSON EIGHT

The Resurrection and the Life

Quick Read

Jesus declared that he was the resurrection and the life and then raised Lazarus to life.

I have stood in cemeteries on cold, windy days with families who have lost loved ones. Their spirits are as gray as the weather around them. Some have expressed a sense of hopelessness and an inability to move ahead with their lives. "What do I do now," they whisper.

I respond, "Jesus said, 'I am the resurrection and the life.'" Maybe the words help. Whatever the case, what we can do in those cemeteries is to do as Jesus did, to shake our fists at death and affirm that death is not the last word. The last word belongs to Jesus, whose death and resurrection conquered death for us all. He is our resurrection and our life.

Jesus had left Jerusalem and was ministering east of the Jordan River when his friend Lazarus became ill. Jesus had gone there because the Jewish authorities had attempted to stone him and were looking for an opportunity to seize him (John 10:39). Jesus had a very special relationship with Lazarus and his two sisters, Mary and Martha (Luke 10:38–42; John 12:1–7).

Mary and Martha recognized the seriousness of Lazarus' illness and sent messengers to tell Jesus (11:3). Although the account records only the message that Lazarus was ill, we can assume that they hoped that Jesus would come and heal him.

Jesus tarried, telling the disciples that the sickness was "not to end in death, but for the glory of God" (11:4). This rather odd statement may be puzzling, for Lazarus did indeed die. We remember, though, that John's Gospel speaks on more than one level. We cannot always identify at first glance on which level Jesus was speaking. We saw this when studying Jesus' conversation with Nicodemus in John 3 and with the Samaritan woman in John 4. Here in 11:4 Jesus evidently was speaking on a level different from the ordinary understanding of the term, "death." Lazarus would die, but Jesus would reverse his death.

Another odd thing about the encounter with the messengers was Jesus' delay in returning to Bethany (11:6), located "about two miles" east of Jerusalem (11:13). We wonder why he did not return immediately and heal Lazarus. No explanation is fully satisfactory. The most obvious and common interpretation is that Lazarus had already died. Thus, Jesus felt no compulsion to return immediately. When he did return, Lazarus had been dead for four days (11:17). If the messengers took one day to travel to Jesus, Jesus waited two more, and then returned on the fourth day, Lazarus was dead when the messengers arrived.

John 11:14–44, 47–53

[14]So Jesus then said to them plainly, "Lazarus is dead, [15]and I am glad for your sakes that I was not there, so that you may believe; but let us go to him." [16]Therefore Thomas, who is called Didymus, said to his fellow disciples, "Let us also go, so that we may die with Him."

[17]So when Jesus came, He found that he had already been in the tomb four days. [18]Now Bethany was near Jerusalem, about two miles off; [19]and many of the Jews had come to Martha and Mary, to console them concerning their brother. [20]Martha therefore, when she heard that Jesus was coming, went to meet Him, but Mary stayed at the house. [21]Martha then said to Jesus, "Lord, if You had been here, my brother would not have died. [22]"Even now I know that whatever You ask of God, God will give You." [23]Jesus said to her, "Your brother will rise again." [24]Martha said to Him, "I know that he will rise again in the resurrection on the last day." [25]Jesus said to her, "I am the resurrection and the life; he who believes in Me will live even if he dies, [26]and everyone who lives and believes in Me will never die. Do you believe this?" [27]She said to Him, "Yes, Lord; I have believed that You are the Christ, the Son of God, even He who comes into the world."

[28]And when she had said this, she went away and called Mary her sister, saying secretly, "The Teacher is here and is calling for you." [29]And when she heard it, she got up quickly and was coming to Him.

[30]Now Jesus had not yet come into the village, but was still in the place where Martha met Him. [31]Then the Jews who were with her in the house, and consoling her, when they saw that Mary got up quickly and went out, they followed her, supposing that she was going to the tomb to weep there. [32]Therefore, when Mary came where Jesus was, she saw Him, and fell at His feet, saying to Him, "Lord, if You had been here, my brother would not have died." [33]When Jesus therefore saw her weeping, and the Jews who came with her also weeping, He was deeply moved in spirit and was troubled, [34]and said, "Where have you laid him?" They said to Him, "Lord, come and see." [35]Jesus wept. [36]So the Jews were saying, "See how He loved him!" [37]But some of them said, "Could not this man, who opened the eyes of the blind man, have kept this man also from dying?"

[38]So Jesus, again being deeply moved within, came to the tomb. Now it was a cave, and a stone was lying against it. [39]Jesus said, "Remove the stone." Martha, the sister of the deceased, said to Him, "Lord, by this time there will be a stench, for he has been dead four days." [40]Jesus said to her, "Did I not say to you that if you believe, you will see the glory of God?" [41]So they removed the stone. Then Jesus raised His eyes, and said,

JOHN: So That You May Believe

"Father, I thank You that You have heard Me. [42]"I knew that You always hear Me; but because of the people standing around I said it, so that they may believe that You sent Me." [43]When He had said these things, He cried out with a loud voice, "Lazarus, come forth." [44]The man who had died came forth, bound hand and foot with wrappings, and his face was wrapped around with a cloth. Jesus said to them, "Unbind him, and let him go."

• •

[47]Therefore the chief priests and the Pharisees convened a council, and were saying, "What are we doing? For this man is performing many signs. [48]"If we let Him go on like this, all men will believe in Him, and the Romans will come and take away both our place and our nation." [49]But one of them, Caiaphas, who was high priest that year, said to them, "You know nothing at all, [50]nor do you take into account that it is expedient for you that one man die for the people, and that the whole nation not perish." [51]Now he did not say this on his own initiative, but being high priest that year, he prophesied that Jesus was going to die for the nation, [52]and not for the nation only, but in order that He might also gather together into one the children of God who are scattered abroad. [53]So from that day on they planned together to kill Him.

Jesus Returns to Bethany (11:14–16)

Jesus told the disciples that Lazarus had died but that he was going to return anyway (11:11). The disciples were not sure this was a good idea (11:12). They remembered that the Jewish leaders had threatened Jesus. To return meant imprisonment and possibly death.

Jesus shared with the apostles that Lazarus' death would provide an occasion through which they might believe in him (11:15). Thomas seems to have spoken for all the disciples when he declared that if Jesus were going to return they might as well return with him and die with him (11:16).

Jesus Arrives at Bethany and Meets Martha (11:17–27)

Jesus arrived in Bethany, met Martha, and was told that Lazarus had been in the tomb for four days. Burial in those days occurred as soon as possible after death, usually on the day of the death. John informs us that many

90

Jews had traveled the two miles or so (literally fifteen *stadia*, or about 9,000 feet) from Jerusalem to mourn with Martha and Mary. That such a large group had come out indicates that Lazarus likely had significant standing and influence in the community.

Martha went out to meet Jesus while Mary remained in the house. Martha has been pictured as the sister of action while the Gospel of John describes Mary as the more reflective sibling (12:2–3; see Luke 10:38–42).

Martha greeted Jesus, calling him "Lord" (11:21). The word is the common term for "sir" and may mean little more than that here. Yet with John's use of multiple levels of meaning, the reader is perhaps to understand

The last word belongs to Jesus, whose death and resurrection conquered death for us all.

that Martha might have been addressing Jesus with the lofty, divine title, "Lord."

Martha commented to Jesus that had he been present Lazarus would not have died (11:21). Some commentators have seen in this a mild rebuke, but most likely it was simply a statement of regret. We can suppose that Martha and Mary had made this comment on several occasions since Lazarus's death. They knew what Jesus could have done although they did not blame him for failing to be present.

Martha's statement that Jesus could have made a difference reveals her faith. Her comment in verse 22 is more difficult. She did not say specifically what she wanted Jesus to ask of God, but what she wanted may have been that God would restore Lazarus to life. Some writers have seen in these words a parallel to the words of Jesus' mother Mary in John 2:5:

In his raising of Lazarus, Jesus would be glorified as the Son of God.

"His mother said to the servants, 'Whatever He says to you, do it.'" Both Martha and Jesus' mother knew the power at Jesus' disposal. Both may have applied subtle hints for him to act to remedy the situation.

Jesus assured Martha that Lazarus would rise from the dead (11:23). Her response indicates that she did not understand what Jesus meant (11:24). She affirmed that Lazarus would rise at the resurrection of all people in the future. Jesus was not the only person who taught a future resurrection. The Pharisees also affirmed a general resurrection.

Jesus' response to Martha's declaration became the focal verse of this conversation. He replied, "I am the resurrection and the life" (11:25).

91

Burial Customs

Burial quickly followed death in ancient Israel. One reason was because of the rapid decomposition of the body. Another reason may have been that contact with a dead body rendered a person ritually unclean (Leviticus 21:1–11; Numbers 6:2–7).

The body was usually prepared for burial by rubbing it with spices and oils. It was then wrapped in a cloth and placed in the tomb. Some graves were natural caves in the hills; others had been cut from the rock or dug out of the ground (see John 19:39–41).

Mourning for the dead was often animated with loud weeping (see Matthew 9:23; John 11:33). Professional mourners could be hired to join family and friends in grieving the loss of loved ones (see Matt. 9:23; Jeremiah 9:17–18).

What Jesus meant is not totally clear. He could not have been referring to the elimination of physical death, for he added, "He who believes in Me will live even if he dies" (11:25). Jesus may not have been speaking of physical resurrection at all, even though he would soon bring Lazarus back to life. Remember the different levels of conversation in John's Gospel (Nicodemus, 3:1–15; the woman at the well, 4:1–26).

Jesus may have been describing the eternal life that is mentioned so often in John. He may have been declaring that in him was a spiritual life that transcended physical existence. People need Jesus more than they need human life. One basis for this interpretation of "I am the resurrection and the life" (11:25) is that Jesus said, "I am," and not *I will be*. In addition, the pronoun "I" is emphatic. Remember the words of Thomas, "Let us also go, so that we may die with Him" (11:16). It was better to die with Jesus than to live without him.

It was better to die with Jesus than to live without him.

Jesus followed this difficult statement in 11:25 by declaring that "everyone who lives and believes in Me will never die" (11:26). He urged Martha, and by implication believers of every age, to trust him.

The most dreaded of all aspects of life is death. Jesus encouraged Martha to trust him completely, even in the death of her brother. When we trust Christ, we experience a life that transcends death. Jesus brought to Martha a present promise and not a future hope only. In Jesus we have eternal and abundant life. Martha's response in 11:27 matches the great confession of Peter found in Matthew 16:16: "You are the Christ, the Son of the living God."

Mary Comes to Jesus (11:28–37)

Martha returned to the house and told Mary that Jesus was asking for her. John's record of the event does not state where and when Jesus made this request. John did not always record everything that transpired during conversations with people. He chose what was necessary for the reader to know and not to satisfy the reader's curiosity. Martha quietly told Mary of Jesus' request because Jesus may have wanted to speak to her alone. Mary quickly arose and went to Jesus. If the purpose of informing Mary in secret was so Jesus could talk with her alone, the plan failed. Those who were grieving with her saw her leave and followed her, thinking she was going to the tomb. Note that Martha called Jesus "the Teacher" when she delivered his summons (11:28).

Mary approached Jesus, voicing the same sentiment that Martha had expressed earlier, "Lord, if you had been here, my brother would not have died" (11:21, 32). Jesus was touched by her grief and sorrow. John describes him as "deeply moved in spirit" and "troubled" (11:33). The word translated "deeply moved" normally means *to groan violently*. It literally means *to snort* and usually indicates some

> *When we trust Christ, we experience a life that transcends death.*

kind of displeasure. He may have been displaying scorn toward those who were offering false comfort to the sisters. More probably Jesus was deeply moved by the pain caused by sickness and death and the struggles they create in human life. The second verb "was troubled" indicates that Jesus was visibly shaken by what he saw. The verbs may simply mean that Jesus was overcome with grief and concern for Mary and Martha.

Jesus asked where Lazarus was buried, and he was taken to the tomb (11:34, 38). He arrived at the grave and was moved by what he saw. John notes that "Jesus wept" (11:25). The term for "wept" contrasts with the term used for Mary and the mourners. They wept loudly, but Jesus wept quietly. Suggestions abound regarding why Jesus wept. Consider these possibilities: (1) He was going to snatch Lazarus from God's presence and return him to this world. (2) He realized that what he was about to do would culminate in his crucifixion. (3) My own view is that he had deep sorrow over the grief of his friends. He cried because they were hurting. This latter interpretation is affirmed by the mourners who saw it. They thought the tears were caused by his deep love for Lazarus. The crowd said (11:37), "Could not this man, who opened the eyes of the blind man, have kept this man also from dying?" They were raising the same concern as that of Martha and Mary (11:21, 32).

Jesus Raises Lazarus (11:37–44)

Jesus and the mourners came to the tomb, a cave with a stone covering the entrance. He instructed the crowd to remove the stone. Martha resisted, reminding him that Lazarus had been dead for four days. Certainly the stench would have been repulsive. The mention of four days implied more than the state of a decomposing body. The Jews believed that the spirit of a dead person hovered around the body for three days following death. The spirit departed on the fourth day. The combination of this belief and the anticipated odor of the body certainly proved that Lazarus was dead. Jesus reminded Martha of what he had told her, that she would "see the glory of God" (11:40).

Christians are people who have staked their lives on Jesus and no other.

"They removed the stone" (11:41). Jesus prayed, thanking God for hearing him. Jesus offered this prayer so that the people would understand that he was not acting on his own. He was thanking God to remind them that he acted as the Father had instructed him to act (11:42; see 8:28–29; 10:37–38). When Jesus finished praying, he shouted, "Lazarus, come forth" (11:43). In a literal translation of the Greek, what Jesus said was, *Here! Outside!* The meaning is, *Leave the tomb and return to the living.*

Lazarus hobbled to the entrance, bound with burial garments. Jesus told them to unbind him. Lazarus was no longer bound by death but was again alive.

The Jewish Authorities Plot Against Jesus (11:47–53)

Many who witnessed the miracle believed in Jesus, but others quickly reported Jesus' actions to the Pharisees. Caiaphas convened the "council"

Martha's Great Confession

Martha's threefold response in John 11:27 shows remarkable insight for one who was not known as being reflective. (1) She affirmed that Jesus was the Christ, God's anointed one. Martha recognized Jesus as the fulfillment of God's promise to send a Messiah. (2) Martha affirmed that Jesus was the Son of God. He was more than simply a chosen person. He possessed a truly unique relationship to God. She recognized the special bond between Father and Son. (3) She also affirmed that Jesus was the person whom God had promised to send into the world to deliver the world. The terms emphasize Martha's commitment to Christ.

to determine how they should respond to the miracle (11:47). The council wondered what they were doing to counter Jesus' popularity. Implied in the question was that they were doing nothing.

They determined that they needed to stop Jesus from acting so boldly. People were following him. Messianic expectations were growing. If the Roman government sensed any type of threat or unrest, they could easily take over the temple and strip the Jewish authorities of all their leadership functions.

Jesus would die not only for the nation but that he might gather people from many nations.

Caiaphas, who was "high priest that year," spoke (11:49). Since he had been high priest since AD 18, "that year" likely refers to the year in which Christ was crucified and not that he was high priest for one year. It was a significant year during his service and for the Jews. He ended the discussion with his rather brusque statement, "You know nothing at all" (11:49). He announced his conclusion that it would be better for one man to die than for the nation to be abolished (11:50).

John interprets Caiaphas' comment from a divine perspective (11:51–52). Caiaphas certainly was not speaking for God when he made the statement, but John stated that Jesus would indeed die for the nation. He would die for the spiritual condition of the people. Further, Jesus would die not only for the nation but that he might gather people from

In Jesus we have eternal and abundant life.

many nations. Caiaphas and the council proceeded on their understanding and grew more intent on discovering how they could kill Jesus.

Implications for Today

In Jesus and in Jesus alone we have life. Christians are people who have staked their lives on Jesus and no other. They are not perfect but have discovered that faith is a growing process. Jesus understands our deepest hurts and responds to our pain. He is our resurrection and our life.

QUESTIONS

1. When have you felt that God failed to respond promptly to your requests?

2. How have you experienced Jesus' promise that he is the resurrection and the life?

3. What can we learn about Jesus from his weeping?

4. What are some events that cause us to grieve besides physical death?

5. When have you felt abandoned by God?

6. Why would the Jewish leaders turn against Jesus after he performed such a marvelous and mighty miracle?

Focal Text

John 11:55–57;
12:20–37, 44–50

Background

John 11:55—12:50

Main Idea

Jesus offered himself to draw all people—including us—to him, challenging us to decide whether we will follow him.

Question to Explore

What does Jesus' offer of himself 2000 years ago mean for you today?

Study Aim

To describe the significance for my life of Jesus' offering himself to draw all people to him

Study and Action Emphases

- Affirm the Bible as our authoritative guide for life and ministry
- Share the gospel with all people
- Develop a growing, vibrant faith

LESSON NINE

The Hour Has Come

Quick Read

Realizing the time had come for him to die, Jesus declared publicly one final time that he was offering himself so that everyone could receive eternal life.

The woman's only son had died. She sought help with her grief, asking the holy man, "What prayers, what magical incantations, do you have to bring my son back to life?" He instructed her to obtain a mustard seed from the home of a family who had never experienced sorrow. She set out, stopping first at the house of someone who was obviously wealthy. "They would never have known sorrow," she thought. She said, as they answered the door, "I am looking for a home that has never known sorrow. Is this such a place? It is very important to me." They began to describe all their tragedies. The woman realized that she could help them because she too had experienced heartache. She stayed to comfort them and then resumed her search.

The woman discovered in every place the pain of sadness and misfortune. She became so involved in ministering that she forgot about her quest for the mustard seed. She forgot about the sorrow that had troubled her own life. She herself became a seed that produced a harvest in others. Jesus, too, offered himself as a seed. He draws all people to himself through his death and resurrection.

John 11:55–57

55Now the Passover of the Jews was near, and many went up to Jerusalem out of the country before the Passover to purify themselves. 56So they were seeking for Jesus, and were saying to one another as they stood in the temple, "What do you think; that He will not come to the feast at all?" 57Now the chief priests and the Pharisees had given orders that if anyone knew where He was, he was to report it, so that they might seize Him.

John 12:20–37, 44–50

20Now there were some Greeks among those who were going up to worship at the feast; 21these then came to Philip, who was from Bethsaida of Galilee, and began to ask him, saying, "Sir, we wish to see Jesus." 22Philip came and told Andrew; Andrew and Philip came and told Jesus. 23And Jesus answered them, saying, "The hour has come for the Son of Man to be glorified. 24"Truly, truly, I say to you, unless a grain of wheat falls into the earth and dies, it remains alone; but if it dies, it bears much fruit. 25"He who loves his life loses it, and he who hates his life in this world will keep it to life eternal. 26"If anyone serves Me, he must follow

Me; and where I am, there My servant will be also; if anyone serves Me, the Father will honor him.

[27]"Now My soul has become troubled; and what shall I say, 'Father, save Me from this hour'? But for this purpose I came to this hour. [28]"Father, glorify Your name." Then a voice came out of heaven: "I have both glorified it, and will glorify it again." [29]So the crowd of people who stood by and heard it were saying that it had thundered; others were saying, "An angel has spoken to Him." [30]Jesus answered and said, "This voice has not come for My sake, but for your sakes. [31]"Now judgment is upon this world; now the ruler of this world will be cast out. [32]"And I, if I am lifted up from the earth, will draw all men to Myself." [33]But He was saying this to indicate the kind of death by which He was to die. [34]The crowd then answered Him, "We have heard out of the Law that the Christ is to remain forever; and how can You say, 'The Son of Man must be lifted up'? Who is this Son of Man?" [35]So Jesus said to them, "For a little while longer the Light is among you. Walk while you have the Light, so that darkness will not overtake you; he who walks in the darkness does not know where he goes. [36]"While you have the Light, believe in the Light, so that you may become sons of Light."

These things Jesus spoke, and He went away and hid Himself from them. [37]But though He had performed so many signs before them, yet they were not believing in Him.

• •

[44]And Jesus cried out and said, "He who believes in Me, does not believe in Me but in Him who sent Me. [45]"He who sees Me sees the One who sent Me. [46]"I have come as Light into the world, so that everyone who believes in Me will not remain in darkness. [47]"If anyone hears My sayings and does not keep them, I do not judge him; for I did not come to judge the world, but to save the world. [48]"He who rejects Me and does not receive My sayings, has one who judges him; the word I spoke is what will judge him at the last day. [49]"For I did not speak on My own initiative, but the Father Himself who sent Me has given Me a commandment as to what to say and what to speak. [50]"I know that His commandment is eternal life; therefore the things I speak, I speak just as the Father has told Me."

The Leaders Plot to Arrest Jesus (11:55–57)

Jesus knew how obsessed the Sanhedrin was to seize him following his restoring Lazarus to life. To avoid the threat, Jesus had journeyed away from Jerusalem, to "the country near the wilderness, into a city called

Ephraim" (11:54). The exact location of Ephraim is uncertain. The time for the Jewish Passover drew near, and the multitudes thronged into Jerusalem. Passover was a popular feast among the Jews and tens of thousands of people might attend during the week's festivities. Attending the feast was important, and people would often come a week early to assure that they were purified for the Thursday night celebration (see Numbers 9:9–14).

The crowds who came were buzzing about Jesus. Three years of public ministry had both attracted converts and created enemies. The curious multitude wanted to see the One who had raised Lazarus. They had heard that the Sanhedrin ("chief priests and Pharisees," 11:57) had issued a warrant for his arrest. These Jewish leaders had commanded that anyone who knew anything about Jesus' whereabouts report it to the authorities. The pilgrims to the feast wondered whether Jesus would appear amid these threats. John phrased their question in a way that suggests they did not expect him to attend.

The coming of the Greeks emphasized that Jesus was a universal Savior.

The Greeks Ask to See Jesus (12:20–26)

Jesus did not disappoint those who hoped to see him. He arrived in Bethany (about two miles from Jerusalem) six days before Passover. During a Saturday night meal hosted by Lazarus, Mary, and Martha, Mary anointed Jesus' feet with expensive perfume. Jesus praised her for anointing him in advance for his coming burial.

Cheering crowds greeted Jesus as the "King of Israel" as he entered Jerusalem the next day (12:13). The manner in which he entered certainly mirrored the way a king would enter. Jesus, however, deliberately chose to ride on a colt to identify himself as a suffering King and not as a conquering war hero. The crowd's enthusiasm prompted the leaders to say that the whole world was following him (12:19).

Some Greeks came to see Jesus. John probably saw in their coming the fulfillment of the unwitting prophecy of the Jewish leaders (see 11:48; 12:19). The Greeks may have been *God-fearers*. God-fearers were non-Jews who were impressed with the high moral standards of Judaism and the worship of only one God. They chose not to become Jewish proselytes through circumcision. Or, rather than being God-fearers, they may simply

God's Voice from Heaven

The New Testament records that God spoke audibly from heaven three times during Jesus' life. The voice came at significant and critical moments in Jesus' ministry. Jesus was either beginning something new or was facing some crisis in which he needed additional affirmation from the Father. In each case the voice affirmed Jesus' work when it conflicted with mistaken notions of those who were present when the voice came.

1. God announced divine approval of Jesus at his baptism. God indicated that Jesus' mission would be that of a suffering servant-king (Matthew 3:17; Mark 1:11; Luke 3:22).

2. Jesus and the inner circle of disciples (Peter, James, John) heard God speak similar words at Jesus' transfiguration. God stressed the importance of the disciples listening to Jesus (Matt. 17:5; Mark 9:7; Luke 9:35).

3. The voice affirmed that Jesus would be glorified in his death (John 12:28).

---

have been non-Jews or Gentiles who had come to Jerusalem for the celebration or to see Jesus. The word translated "now" may contrast the Greeks with unbelieving Jewish leaders like the Pharisees (12:19).

The Greeks expressed to Philip a desire "to see Jesus" (12:21). To "see" meant more than to *look at*. They could have done that without consulting Philip. They wanted to visit with Jesus. Some commentators suggest that the word here may imply *to believe in* him. Philip found Andrew, and together they told Jesus about the request. It is unclear why the Greeks went to Philip, although both he and Andrew had Greek names. The Gospel of John points out that Philip came from Bethsaida in Galilee, an area where many Gentiles lived (1:44).

Whether Jesus actually spoke with the Greeks is unclear. The word "them" (12:23) could refer either to the Greeks or to Philip and Andrew. Jesus probably spoke specifically to Philip and Andrew with the Greeks and others who were nearby listening to him as he spoke.

> *As the Father . . . would honor the Son because of his service, so the Father would honor those who followed and served Christ (12:26).*

Jesus' response to the request seems odd and abrupt. The Greeks had sought an audience, but Jesus appeared to ignore their request. Looking at the broad context of his mission helps us to understand why. He asserted that his mission would lead to his death. In John's Gospel, being "glorified" (12:23) always points to the whole event of Jesus' crucifixion, resurrection, and ascension. While people might view Jesus' death as a tragic event, the Gospel of John asserts that it was a time of glory for Jesus and the Father. Jesus understood the Gentiles' interest in his work as an indication that his work was nearly complete. The coming of the Greeks emphasized that Jesus was a universal Savior.

We cannot minimize the degree to which Jesus suffered for us.

Jesus' reply may have been a more direct response than we at first realize, for the only way to truly "see" him is through eyes of faith in his glorification. The verb "has come" stresses that the time had arrived and would remain until completed (12:23). There was no turning back.

Jesus used the agricultural image of a seed to illustrate his understanding of his work. A seed is planted. It dies. In its death, it is reborn as a plant that grows and produces a much greater harvest than the one original seed. The Son of Man, like the seed, must die to achieve a great harvest.

Jesus next explained that one must *hate* this earthly life to obtain eternal life. The word "loses" can be translated *destroys* (12:25). Understanding the word in this manner makes a powerful statement. The first word rendered "life" is the Greek word for *soul* and normally means *individual personality* (12:25). People lose this life when they place the matters of this world above eternal matters. "Hates" does not mean *detest* but is used as a contrast with love (12:23). Jesus was saying that the one whose priorities were in this world and not the eternal world would not have eternal life, God's kind of life, which begins now, in this age. Parallels to this statement can be found in other gospels (Matthew 10:39; Mark 8:36; Luke 14:26).

What the world would see as a wasted effort, Christ transformed into victory over Satan.

The one who "hates" this earthly life would be the one who served Christ and followed him as a disciple. Jesus emphasized that he was the focus of the disciples' allegiance and commitment. His disciples would find themselves in the places and situations like those in which Christ found himself. He specifically meant that disciples would face their own cross and suffering. As the Father, however, would honor the Son because of his service, so the Father would honor those who followed and served Christ (12:26).

Jesus Commits Himself to His Death (12:27–37)

The allusion to his death "troubled" Jesus (12:27). His awareness of his impending passion likely increased as the time for its realization drew near. He understood that he would suffer as his followers would later suffer. His anguish described here finds a parallel in the synoptic gospel accounts of his struggling in the Garden of Gethsemane (Matt. 26:36–46; Mark 14:32–42; Luke 22:39–46). We can interpret John 12:27 in two ways, but both express the idea that Jesus was wrestling with the task that lay before him. He either (1) prayed or (2) contemplated praying that God would deliver him from that hour. No matter which choice you prefer, Jesus' next words, "but for this purpose I came to this hour," affirm that he came to die so that the world might have the eternal life he offered. We should certainly see in this verse Jesus' personal agony and struggle as he anticipated what awaited him. We cannot minimize the degree to which Jesus suffered for us. His struggle with knowing and doing God's will unquestionably testifies to his humanity.

Jesus expressed his resolve to do the Father's will and then asked the Father to glorify the divine name (12:28). A voice boomed from heaven, declaring that the Father indeed had glorified the name. God would do so again in the future, at Jesus' crucifixion. The nearby crowd heard the voice, but most of them thought they had heard thunder (12:29). Others, perhaps more aware of what was happening in Jesus' life, declared that it was an angel's voice. Apparently no one but Jesus understood the words. Jesus explained to the multitude that the voice had come for their sakes, for they needed the divine witness. Jesus knew he was following the Father's will.

The idea of judgment appears as Jesus reflected on his glorification (12:31). His crucifixion would demonstrate God's power over the evil one. It would also show the triumph of faith in God over love for this world. Satan had worked to derail Christ's ministry from the outset, from Herod's effort to kill the child-king (Matt. 2:1–12) to Jesus' questioning the necessity of his death (John 12:27). What the world would see as a wasted effort, Christ transformed into victory over Satan.

Jesus announced that he would be "lifted up" (12:32). This verb is used in John's Gospel only to refer to Jesus' death (see 3:14; 8:28; 12:32, 34). It is translated "exalt" in other places in the New Testament (Luke 14:11; 18:14). Jesus' usage here may be another instance in John where a word carries two meanings. Jesus would be lifted up on a cross and in that manner of death would be exalted. Jesus would draw "all men"—all people—to him in his death (12:32). Everyone will not be saved, but no one is left out because of ethnicity. Greeks (12:20) as well as Jews could believe.

The crowd failed to grasp Jesus' meaning (12:34). They believed the Messiah ("Christ," *the anointed one*) would live forever. They used the title "Son of Man" when they questioned Jesus. The emphatic pronouns "we" and "You" strongly contrast the two understandings of the Messiah's work. The crowd cited the "Law" that the Messiah would remain forever. "Law" refers to all the Old Testament Scripture. No one passage is directly quoted, but several allude to this concept (see Psalm 89:36; Ezekiel 37:25; Isaiah 9:7).

The people wanted Jesus to explain the Messiah's role to them (John 12:34). He did so indirectly. When Jesus reminded them that the light was still with them, he may have been referring to earlier statements he had made (John 8:12; 9:5). Travelers journey while light remains. Jesus taught the people that they must recognize that he is the light and learn of him while he was still alive. When darkness sets in, people cannot see where they are going. As long as Jesus was

> Everyone will not be saved, but no one is left out because of ethnicity.

with them, they were in the presence of the light. They should believe in him before he departed so that they would become "sons of Light" (12:36). The belief that Jesus demanded was a continuous trust in him. Those who responded to this invitation would have the character of light. They would become like Christ as his disciples.

The Gospel of John tells us that Jesus "hid Himself" (12:36). He may have gone into hiding to prevent the authorities from arresting him, but the passage does not say. John may have simply been saying that Jesus had ended his public ministry. Jesus devoted himself to his disciples in the remainder of the book. He had worked many miracles and performed many signs, but people were not trusting him and following him as disciples. John 1:11 spoke of this earlier, saying: "He came to His own, and those who were His own did not receive Him."

Jesus Appeals to the People One Final Time (12:44–50)

John was not surprised that the people had refused to believe. The Old Testament had stated that people would reject God (see Isaiah 6:9–10).

Passover

The Gospel of John mentions three Passover feasts during Jesus' public ministry. Matthew, Mark, and Luke mention only the last. John's Gospel enriches the synoptic account of Jesus' public ministry. These are the three Passovers that John mentions:

1. The first Passover is the one in which Jesus drove the merchants and money changers from the temple (2:13–25).
2. The second Passover in John is the one at which Jesus fed the 5,000 in Galilee (6:4). By this miracle he associated himself with the giving of life to the nation. John does not record Jesus' visiting Jerusalem at this time.
3. The third Passover is the one at which time Jesus was arrested, tried, convicted, and crucified (11:55).

People had always witnessed the power and concern for God in their lives and refused to turn to the Lord. The people who witnessed the life and teachings of the Son likewise rejected the Son's message of eternal life.

One final time, Jesus cried out to the crowd in a loud voice. He ended his public ministry by summing up his teachings on these topics: (1) people believing in him; (2) Jesus' being sent by the Father; (3) people facing judgment because of how they received Jesus; and (4) eternal life being found in the Father.

To "believe in" Jesus meant to entrust themselves to the Son (12:44). To entrust themselves to the Son meant they were also entrusting themselves to the Father. To see and comprehend the identity of the Son was to see and comprehend the Father who sent the Son.

Jesus reserved harsh words for those who rejected him. He did not claim that he would judge them, because he had not come to condemn. He came to give life to people. He offered them a new way, the way of eternal life through himself. However, those who refused to believe in Jesus faced judgment. His "word" would be their judge (12:48). The word was truth, light, and life. When those who reject Christ stand at the last day, they will hear again the words that promised life, and they will remember they had rejected those words.

God's commandment is life, the life that Jesus proclaimed in word and offered through his sacrificial death for all people.

Jesus reminded them that he spoke, not on his own initiative, but at the command of the Father. The Son's words were the Father's words. Jesus obediently proclaimed the divine message to the people. The commandment—the message—was eternal life. Jesus did not say that keeping the commandment produces eternal life. Neither does the commandment simply talk about eternal life. Rather, the commandment itself is "eternal life" (12:50). God's word for us is not law but grace. God's word for us is not judgment, but mercy. God's word for us is not confining, but liberating. God's commandment is life, the life that Jesus proclaimed in word and offered through his sacrificial death for all people. The word demands a decision. Will you accept or reject Christ's offer of eternal life?

> God's word for us is not law but grace.

QUESTIONS

1. What would you do if you knew that you had only one week to live? How do your thoughts compare with Jesus' actions in these Scriptures?

2. What things in this world do you love? How could loving these keep you from obtaining eternal life?

3. What reasons do people give for choosing not to follow Jesus?

4. How do your ideas about Jesus compare or contrast with the picture of him as one who must suffer?

5. What does Jesus' statement that those who serve him must follow him in their own cross experience mean to you?

6. Does Jesus ever stop drawing people to himself?

Jesus' Glorious Triumph

As a little girl, I didn't own a red-letter edition of the Bible, but a friend did. I was jealous of her beautifully colored Scripture pages. I remember wondering why the beginning of the Bible didn't have any words printed in red. Then, as I turned the pages of the Bible, I noticed lots of red ink and finally none at the end. Margaret Rountree, a wise children's teacher at First Baptist Church of Eldorado, Texas, explained to me that the red indicated words Jesus spoke. She told me that while Jesus said them to his followers then, Jesus also means them for us now.

Today, I own a red-letter edition of the Bible, and I notice that every chapter in John contains the words of Jesus. He reveals himself to us through what he says and what he does.

Unit Four is a study of Scriptures selected from John 13—21 and deals with Jesus' farewell instructions, his crucifixion, and his resurrection appearances.

The Savior's teachings fill chapters 13—17, the first two lessons of the unit, as Jesus prepared the disciples for their earthly life after his earthly death. Lesson ten explores John 13 and Jesus' example of service and love by washing the disciples' feet at their last meal together.

Lesson eleven treats Scriptures from John 14—17 and considers Jesus' parting discourse to his followers. As Jesus moved closer to the cross, he comforted his disciples as they faced life without his earthly presence. God's Son promised the presence of the Spirit in his absence and offered encouragement and strength as he prayed for himself, the disciples, and all believers.

In chapters 18—19, the Gospel of John portrays the events leading up to the crucifixion and describes Jesus' death on the cross. Lesson twelve focuses on Jesus' willingness to fulfill his mission of drawing all people to his salvation.

Lesson thirteen provides a study of Scripture selections from John 20—21, emphasizing God's confirmation of Jesus' identity through the empty tomb, the resurrection appearances, and the testimony of changed lives. As Jesus prepared to return to heaven, he commissioned all believers, including us, to be witnesses for him on earth.

The chapters in the unit are familiar to most Christians. However, as I read them again for these lessons, I tried to put myself in the place of the disciples who heard Jesus' teachings for the first time and who watched his actions as eyewitnesses. I invite you to study these passages with the freshness of the disciples' eyes.[1]

UNIT FOUR, JESUS' GLORIOUS TRIUMPH

NOTES

1. Unless otherwise indicated, all Scripture quotations in Unit Four are from The Holy Bible, New International Version (North American Edition), copyright © 1973, 1978, 1984 by the International Bible Society. Used by permission of Zondervan Publishing House.

Focal Text

John 13:1–17

Background

John 13:1–30

Main Idea

As Jesus approached his death, he provided us an example of humble service that is to characterize the lives of Christians, too.

Question to Explore

When do you do as Jesus did in washing the disciples' feet?

Study Aim

To identify ways I will follow Jesus' example of service

Study and Action Emphases

- Affirm the Bible as our authoritative guide for life and ministry
- Share the gospel with all people
- Develop a growing, vibrant faith
- Obey and serve Jesus by meeting physical, spiritual, and emotional needs
- Equip people for servant leadership

LESSON TEN

Do As Jesus Did

Quick Read

Washing the disciples' feet beautifully illustrates the humble service and love that Jesus expected from his followers after his death and asks from us today.

Our family and college friends watch with interest when movies directed by Kevin Reynolds premiere. Kevin, son of former Baylor University President Herbert H. Reynolds, grew up in Texas Baptist churches and graduated from Baylor with both undergraduate and law degrees. But he dreamed of Hollywood, where he has directed such movies as *Robin Hood: Prince of Thieves* and *The Count of Monte Cristo*.

My husband and I especially enjoy Kevin's movies set in the distant past. The history major in him leads to meticulous research of the customs of the period. The director in him requires that the characters become immersed in the time. Only when heritage comes together with story does the movie become an artistic portrait of the past that expands the horizons of the audience.

Similar thoughts hold true of John 13. An understanding of the setting and customs of the time enhances the word pictures and characters in the biblical drama we know as the Last Supper. The Gospel of John doesn't mention the Lord's Supper itself, however, possibly because John was the last of the four gospels written and Christians already were celebrating the ordinance.

A Portrait of Heritage and Horizon (13:1)

The Gospel of John states, "Having loved his own who were in the world, he now showed them the full extent of his love" (13:1). Jesus' hour had come. Jesus reminded the disciples of the heritage of that love even as he prepared them for his love's completion on the horizon.

During their final meal together, Jesus demonstrated the completeness, consistency, and constancy of his love for his followers through his hospitality, humility, and honesty. In turn, our Lord expects his own to demonstrate that same kind of love to others in spite of their and our humanity.

A Portrait of Hospitality and Honor (13:2–5)

As the new, inexperienced Woman's Missionary Union director for our church, I didn't know what to do. Then several mission leaders with children near my age took me under their wings and insisted I attend WMU week at Glorieta Baptist Conference Center in New Mexico with them. The three women awed me. Texas WMU officers Dorothy Lamberth and

John 13:1–17

¹It was just before the Passover Feast. Jesus knew that the time had come for him to leave this world and go to the Father. Having loved his own who were in the world, he now showed them the full extent of his love.

²The evening meal was being served, and the devil had already prompted Judas Iscariot, son of Simon, to betray Jesus. ³Jesus knew that the Father had put all things under his power, and that he had come from God and was returning to God; ⁴so he got up from the meal, took off his outer clothing, and wrapped a towel around his waist. ⁵After that, he poured water into a basin and began to wash his disciples' feet, drying them with the towel that was wrapped around him.

⁶He came to Simon Peter, who said to him, "Lord, are you going to wash my feet?"

⁷Jesus replied, "You do not realize now what I am doing, but later you will understand."

⁸"No," said Peter, "you shall never wash my feet."

Jesus answered, "Unless I wash you, you have no part with me."

⁹"Then, Lord," Simon Peter replied, "not just my feet but my hands and my head as well!"

¹⁰Jesus answered, "A person who has had a bath needs only to wash his feet; his whole body is clean. And you are clean, though not every one of you." ¹¹For he knew who was going to betray him, and that was why he said not every one was clean.

¹²When he had finished washing their feet, he put on his clothes and returned to his place. "Do you understand what I have done for you?" he asked them. ¹³"You call me 'Teacher' and 'Lord,' and rightly so, for that is what I am. ¹⁴Now that I, your Lord and Teacher, have washed your feet, you also should wash one another's feet. ¹⁵I have set you an example that you should do as I have done for you. ¹⁶I tell you the truth, no servant is greater than his master, nor is a messenger greater than the one who sent him. ¹⁷Now that you know these things, you will be blessed if you do them.

Wilma Reed, former missionary Ann Pitman, and I crowded into a small apartment at the conference center.

We cooked our own meals and enjoyed the conversation and camaraderie that cramped quarters afford. Although I didn't know anyone at the conference, the other women knew everyone, and our home-away-from-home became a gathering place. The three offered iced tea, water, or coffee to their friends who stopped by. Then I ran into a college friend. Ann insisted she come for supper. I knew we didn't have enough food, but when Mary Ann appeared, she received royal treatment. Years later, Mary Ann reminded me of the unselfish gift of hospitality and how we should have been waiting on these women. My friend also had noticed that we received larger portions of food on our plates than did others.

Today, we offer our guests cool or warm drinks and something to eat when they appear. We direct them to a place where they can wash their hands and freshen up. In Jesus' day, guests needed something different. In first-century Palestine, guests needed their feet washed. The people went barefoot or wore sandals to walk through streets shared with animals and their byproducts. Feet got dirty and smelly, even on short journeys. Footwashing offered both cleanliness and refreshment. Usually a slave or the lowest servant in the household washed guests' feet, although Jewish slaves were exempt from the offensive task. Occasionally the host's wife performed the act of hospitality. Obviously removing the manure-mixed dirt was demeaning, certainly not a task for a host or master.

Jesus washed the disciples' feet, not because he had to but because he wanted to.

Jesus gathered his disciples for a final meal together just before Passover. He knew he would soon leave the earth to be with his Father. Just as we particularly value time with family and friends before we move away or with our children before they empty our nests, Jesus made every moment precious with the disciples. The disciples were human, though, seeking power and glory. They squabbled about "which of them was considered to be greatest" (Luke 22:24).

. . . We should honestly follow Christ's model as we conquer pride and perform whatever service the Master assigns.

No slaves or servants were present, and no one offered the hospitality of washing feet. While disciples of the time performed many small tasks for their masters, they drew the line at removing sandals and footwashing. The greatest could never wash another person's feet. Doing so would offer proof of being the least important person in the group.

Dinner had already begun when Jesus got up. At the Passover meal, hosts and guests gathered around a low table. So they could eat with their right hands, they lay on their left sides with their heads propped up on their elbows and their legs stretched out. The guest of honor reclined to

"Father" R. C. Buckner: A Servant Leader

Those who knew him said Baptist minister Robert Cooke Buckner possessed a heart big enough for every orphan. In 1879, R. C. and his wife Vienna opened an orphanage in Dallas, Texas, with three children. The three grew to hundreds, but Vienna and R. C. didn't just run the orphanage. They also raised the funds, sometimes giving personal notes to pay the bills.

One of the stories told of Buckner's ministry that illustrates his view of service is of a little girl whose family died in a fire that left her badly burned. When "Father" Buckner returned from his frequent train trips, the children always wanted to kiss him. One day, Mary cried while she watched. Buckner walked over and asked why she didn't come to him. Tears welled as Mary said she couldn't ask him to kiss her because she was so ugly. But if he could just love her, he didn't need to kiss her. Buckner leaned down and gently kissed her scarred face.

When Buckner lay dying, he reportedly asked, "Please do not fold my hands. Leave them open, ready for work." Today, close to 125 years later, Father Buckner's legacy of unselfish service to children lives on through Buckner Baptist Benevolences.[1]

---

the right of the host. At this supper, "the disciple whom Jesus loved," generally considered to be John himself, held that position where he could see and hear all the events of the evening (John 13:23). He watched as Jesus took off his outer garment and wrapped a towel around his waist (13:4).

Then Jesus poured water into a bowl. Around the circle, Jesus knelt beside the disciples in turn, removing their sandals. Then Jesus gently washed and dried each one's filthy feet (13:5).

Jesus charged his disciples and us today to be his willing servant-messengers in and to the world.

Jesus washed the disciples' feet, not because he had to but because he wanted to. No one did that. Christ defined himself, not with a crown and a throne but with a basin and a towel. He chose to make himself nothing and in so doing showed himself to be the greatest of all (see Philippians 2:7–11).

A Portrait of Humility and Humiliation (13:6–11)

Several years ago bumper stickers and jewelry with the letters *WWJD* on them became the rage. Texas Baptists used the theme "What Would Jesus

Do?" for an annual Week of Prayer for Texas Missions. For several months following the emphasis, when the first- through sixth-grade girls in Girls in Action (GAs) I worked with faced a problem or difficult issue, they looked at one another or at a mission leader and asked, "WWJD?"

What will we choose—a crown of glory or a towel of service?

Perhaps, though, the answers would have been clearer if the question had been *WDJD?* for *What Did Jesus Do?*

The Apostle Peter could easily have answered that question. As an eyewitness, he would say, *Jesus humbled himself, and I felt humiliated.* At the farewell supper, Jesus finally came to the impetuous Simon Peter. In amazement, the disciple blurted out (13:6), "Lord, are you going to wash my feet?"

The answer was obvious. Jesus would wash Peter's feet just as he had washed the others' feet. Jesus, however, didn't answer, *Yes.* Instead he gently explained that Peter didn't understand Jesus' actions now, but he would later (13:7).

Peter still didn't get it. He responded that Jesus would *never* wash his feet. The stubborn apostle couldn't have been more emphatic with his rejection. The Messiah insisted, though, "Unless I wash you, you have no part with me" (13:8).

Peter needed to swallow his pride. He needed to allow himself the humiliation of having his feet washed by his Master so that he, too, could become a servant leader.

Peter's impetuous mood swung predictably. If he needed his feet clean, why not let Jesus wash his hands and head, too? In other words, just bathe me all over (13:9).

Perhaps Jesus' eyes twinkled and his mouth twitched, almost in a smile.

Jesus indicated that we will be happy if we do what he shows us to do.

Customarily before such dinners, the participants bathed. Only their feet became dusty on the trip to the upper room. The Savior continued the lesson of humility and humiliation by saying, "A person who has had a bath needs only to wash his feet; his whole body is clean" (13:10). Only renewal, refreshing, and recommitment were necessary after the initial cleansing.

Then Jesus' face probably reflected somber sadness as he added, "And you are clean, though not every one of you" (13:10). He knew that Judas did not share with the other disciples the cleanliness of the faith in him as the Messiah (13:11).

A Portrait of Honesty and Happiness (13:12–17)

Through the years I've collected scores of bags from conventions and conferences. One of my favorites pictures a bright orange logo on a sturdy black zipper tote. A stylized person with a towel draped over the person's arms kneels in front of an outline of the world. Bold letters add the words, "SERVE in Christ's name."

As Christians today, we must be examples as we follow Christ's example.

Jesus painted the portrait, but he had to be sure the disciples knew the meaning, *SERVE in my name.* He put on his outer clothing, returned to his place at the table, and asked (13:12), "Do you understand what I have done for you?" Before they could answer, the Savior explained that he rightly held the position of Teacher and Lord. He deserved their worship, their respect, and their devotion. Further, he should be their example. Since he washed their feet, they should wash others' feet (13:13–15).

Since Jesus' words not only apply to the Twelve but also to us as his disciples today, did Jesus literally mean that we should wash one another's feet? Was he adding a third ordinance to baptism and the Lord's Supper? No, although some denominations do practice footwashing as a symbol of Christ's service. Instead, Jesus said that he had set an example with his act (13:15). An example is a model that deserves imitation. The disciples and we should honestly follow Christ's model as we conquer pride and perform whatever service the Master assigns.

Christ defined himself, not with a crown and a throne but with a basin and a towel.

Jesus said, "No servant is greater than his master, nor is a messenger greater than the one who sent him" (13:16). For servants to become great, they must be willing to render whatever service the Master requires and to do it well. For messengers to be effective, they must carry with speed and accuracy the words of the one who sends them.

Jesus charged his disciples and us today to be his willing servant-messengers in and to the world. He said, "Now that you know these things,

"Divine Servant"

A bronze sculpture stands outside the student center at Dallas Baptist University. The statue portrays Jesus washing a disciple's feet as it reinforces the university's mission "to produce servant leaders." How can we become servant leaders? Consider these ideas and add to them:

- Offer pedicures or manicures in a nursing home or to the homeless
- Work on a Habitat for Humanity house or help a family repair their home
- Teach someone to read
- Prepare a weekend meal for children whose only food comes from their school's free lunches and breakfasts
- Participate in a mission trip to an overseas orphanage where you rock babies and change their diapers with love

you will be blessed if you do them" (13:17). "Blessed" is the same word Jesus used in the Beatitudes (Matthew 5:3–12) and may be translated *happy*. In other words, Jesus indicated that we will be happy if we do what he shows us to do. As Christians today, we must be examples as we follow Christ's example.

A Portrait of the Here and Hereafter

Marv Knox, editor of the *Baptist Standard*, says his mother knew the importance of being an example. He grew up as a preacher's son and recalls his mother's frequent admonition when he left the parsonage, "Don't do anything that would ruin your daddy's ministry." As parents, John and I gave similar instructions. Before Marshall, Michael, and Holly visited grandparents or friends, we encouraged them to be "better than perfect." We figured that if they tried for perfection they wouldn't do too much wrong.

> I can almost hear the Savior whisper, Don't do anything that would ruin your Heavenly Father's ministry.

Sometimes when we squabble over power, money, and who will be the greatest in our churches and denomination, I can almost hear the Savior whisper, *Don't do anything that would ruin your Heavenly Father's ministry. Instead, show your love for each other and for the lost by your willingness to kneel and wash their feet. The true measure of greatness lies not in where you sit but in how you serve.*

Jesus' example added the final brush stroke to the portrait of how the disciples should live as servant leaders in the here and now when the Master moved to the hereafter. The question for us is the same they faced. How will we live? What will we choose—a crown of glory or a towel of service? Will we do as Jesus did?

QUESTIONS

1. What do you think keeps Christians from serving in the way Jesus taught?

2. How can Christians today follow Jesus' example of service?

3. Why don't most Baptist churches regularly practice footwashing?

4. What are some qualities of a servant leader?

5. How do we obey and serve Jesus by meeting physical, spiritual, and emotional needs?

6. How can we model humble service to preschoolers, children, teens, and college students?

NOTES

1.   See Harry Leon McBeth, *Texas Baptists: A Sesquicentennial History* (Dallas, Texas: BAPTISTWAY PRESS, 1998), 73.

Focal Text

John 14:15–27;
15:26—16:15

Background

John 13:31—17:26

Main Idea

Jesus continues to provide encouragement and strength for Christian living to all who turn to him.

Question to Explore

How can you face challenges to and concerns about your faith?

Study Aim

To describe implications for my life of the sources of encouragement and strength for Christian living identified in these Scriptures

Study and Action Emphases

- Affirm the Bible as our authoritative guide for life and ministry
- Share the gospel with all people
- Develop a growing, vibrant faith
- Include all God's family in decision-making and service
- Value all people as created in the image of God

LESSON ELEVEN

Never Alone

Quick Read

As Jesus moved closer to the cross, he comforted his disciples, promised the presence of the Holy Spirit in his absence, and offered encouragement and strength through his prayers.

As a college student I spent two summers counseling at a girls' camp on the Guadalupe River in the Texas Hill Country. Because I edited the camp newspaper, early Friday mornings saw me driving an aging station wagon into Kerrville to proofread and complete the layout. One Thursday, rain dampened the normal outdoor activities. From time to time Thursday night, I woke to claps of thunder and the patter of rain on the cabin's tile roof. I rose before reveille, grabbed the keys, and headed to the kitchen for a quick cup of coffee. The camp owners' brother beat me there and urged me to delay my trip until daylight. A few minutes later, the kitchen phone rang. A friend upriver warned that a dangerous flood was headed our way.

Billy went to postpone reveille and check on the horses. I ran to wake up counselors, sending some to move equipment out of a gully and others to the waterfront to rescue canoes. With the last of the boats almost put away, a wall of water roared down the Guadalupe carrying tree limbs, camp equipment, furniture, animals, and anything in its path. In that helpless, hopeless moment, there was nothing anyone could do to divert the raging river.

Jesus knew that his followers would feel that same kind of hopeless helplessness as Judas Iscariot set in motion the raging river of events that would lead to the crucifixion. On the evening before his death, the Savior delivered his farewell discourse.

John 14:15–27

[15]"If you love me, you will obey what I command. [16]And I will ask the Father, and he will give you another Counselor to be with you forever— [17]the Spirit of truth. The world cannot accept him, because it neither sees him nor knows him. But you know him, for he lives with you and will be in you. [18]I will not leave you as orphans; I will come to you. [19]Before long, the world will not see me anymore, but you will see me. Because I live, you also will live. [20]On that day you will realize that I am in my Father, and you are in me, and I am in you. [21]Whoever has my commands and obeys them, he is the one who loves me. He who loves me will be loved by my Father, and I too will love him and show myself to him."

[22]Then Judas (not Judas Iscariot) said, "But, Lord, why do you intend to show yourself to us and not to the world?"

[23]Jesus replied, "If anyone loves me, he will obey my teaching. My Father will love him, and we will come to him and make our home with

him. 24He who does not love me will not obey my teaching. These words you hear are not my own; they belong to the Father who sent me.

25"All this I have spoken while still with you. 26But the Counselor, the Holy Spirit, whom the Father will send in my name, will teach you all things and will remind you of everything I have said to you. 27Peace I leave with you; my peace I give you. I do not give to you as the world gives. Do not let your hearts be troubled and do not be afraid."

John 15:26–27

26"When the Counselor comes, whom I will send to you from the Father, the Spirit of truth who goes out from the Father, he will testify about me. 27And you also must testify, for you have been with me from the beginning.

John 16:1–15

1"All this I have told you so that you will not go astray. 2They will put you out of the synagogue; in fact, a time is coming when anyone who kills you will think he is offering a service to God. 3They will do such things because they have not known the Father or me. 4I have told you this, so that when the time comes you will remember that I warned you. I did not tell you this at first because I was with you.

5"Now I am going to him who sent me, yet none of you asks me, 'Where are you going?' 6Because I have said these things, you are filled with grief. 7But I tell you the truth: It is for your good that I am going away. Unless I go away, the Counselor will not come to you; but if I go, I will send him to you. 8When he comes, he will convict the world of guilt in regard to sin and righteousness and judgment: 9in regard to sin, because men do not believe in me; 10in regard to righteousness, because I am going to the Father, where you can see me no longer; 11and in regard to judgment, because the prince of this world now stands condemned.

12"I have much more to say to you, more than you can now bear. 13But when he, the Spirit of truth, comes, he will guide you into all truth. He will not speak on his own; he will speak only what he hears, and he will tell you what is yet to come. 14He will bring glory to me by taking from what is mine and making it known to you. 15All that belongs to the Father is mine. That is why I said the Spirit will take from what is mine and make it known to you."

Challenge (13:31–38)

Farewell discourses weren't unusual in the ancient world. The Bible records those of Jacob (Genesis 49), Joshua (Joshua 23—24), David (1 Chronicles 28—29), and Moses (Deuteronomy 31—33). Typically the farewell was spoken to a gathering of family or followers and began with an announcement of imminent death. The speaker offered promises and blessings before reviewing his or her life. The dying person named successors, left final instructions, and closed in prayer. Jesus' last teachings to his disciples followed a similar pattern. They provided all of his followers of all generations with glimpses into the Savior's heart and soul.

In that helpless, hopeless moment, there was nothing anyone could do to divert the raging river.

The eleven disciples lingered after the Last Supper. Jesus told them he would soon glorify God through his death and go to a place where they could not come. He addressed them as his children and commanded them, "As I have loved you, so you must love one another" (John 13:31). Not only would the disciples need to rely on one another for strength, but also the world would see Jesus' love in them and know they belonged to him (13:35). Love for fellow believers would be the standard by which the world judged Christians. So it remains today.

The ever-impulsive Simon Peter interjected his promise to die for the Master. However, before the night watch ended, he would deny the Savior three times (13:37–38). Peter and the others could not be with Christ during those last hours. Jesus knew he had to walk the final moments alone. So, ahead of time, he offered his followers comfort, counsel, and communication with the Heavenly Father as they faced the challenge of the change brought by his death on the cross.

Comfort (14:15–27)

Almost fifteen years after the flood I experienced as a camp counselor, I reflected back on that experience. What if I had been on the road at a low water crossing when the waters roared down? Would I have survived? God blessed us with a flood before sunrise. The only living thing we lost was a favorite camp horse. The animal crossed the Guadalupe at a shallow spot

The Youth-Led Revival Movement

In 1944, several hundred students gathered at Baylor University's Baptist Student Union retreat. As the embers of a campfire burned to close a powerful day, about fifteen young men lingered. Reiji Hoshizaki, a Japanese-American, and M. D. Oates, a tennis player, wanted to hold a campus revival. The group began praying nightly and set an April date.

With encouragement from their Baptist Student Union director, the students raised $1,100. Attendance topped 3,000 each night. Two hundred eighty-one made commitments as the students sang, shared testimonies, and preached. Prayer and planning immediately began for the 1946 revival, where about 500 made decisions.

Soon new BSU director W. J. Wimpee received an invitation for the students to lead revival in Houston. He sensed the Holy Spirit moving, and the students asked Dr. W. F. Howard, director of Texas Baptists' student work, to handle mushrooming requests. From 1946 through 1962, more than 1,500 youth-led revivals resulted in 55,000 public commitments.

How did such a small group with little training begin a movement that achieved such miraculous results? The Holy Spirit walked alongside them, taught them, witnessed for them, revealed how to put action to faith, and brought conviction for decision.

but couldn't return when the river rose. As best we could, we comforted her owner and the campers who loved the mare.

All those memories returned as I watched the news on July 17, 1987. With our oldest son at a boys' camp down the road from where I counseled, I heard the words, "Guadalupe River" and "flood." A rapid rise—ironically, near Comfort, Texas—stranded a bus and van belonging to Seagoville Road Baptist Church as the students hurriedly left church camp. Ten of the forty-three passengers died in the floodwaters. As I listened to interviews of parents, church leaders, and survivors, I glimpsed the kind of comfort and hope that Jesus gave his disciples as he prepared to leave the earth.

The Spirit does not give new truth, but, as with the disciples, the Spirit enables us to grow in understanding God.

The Savior's words, "Do not let your hearts be troubled," offered comfort to the disciples (14:1). They still do. Jesus also provided the greatest comfort of all. He promised the Holy Spirit. But like most biblical promises,

Jesus created a condition. "If you love me, you will obey what I command" (14:15). In other words, we must love and obey Jesus. Then, Christ said he would pray to the Father for another Comforter who would live in and with his followers as the "Spirit of truth" forever (14:16–17). Jesus took the role of Divine Helper. The Spirit would be another of the same kind as Jesus. But the Spirit's being with us would be tied to our love and obedience.

In this first of Jesus' five teachings in John 14—16 about the Holy Spirit, the disciples began to understand how the Comforter would minister to them (see 14:16–17; 14:26; 15:26; 16:7–11; 16:13–15). The Spirit would be their Helper. Bible translators use various words for the Greek word *parakletos*, which literally means, *the one called alongside*. Choices include Advocate, Counselor, Helper, Comforter, Encourager, or the transliterated word Paraclete. In secular Greek, *parakletos* simply meant one called to help as a friend at court, serving as a legal adviser, helper, and advocate. Like a defense lawyer who serves as an advocate for one accused, the Paraclete stands ready to walk alongside and help the Christian through the difficult circumstances of life.

> In spite of the dangerous river of events flowing around him, Jesus experienced and offered peace as he led his disciples out of the upper room (14:31).

As the disciples suffered opposition and hostility from the world, Jesus promised unconditionally, "I will not leave you as orphans" (14:18). They would live because the Savior would live after his crucifixion. They would know that "I am in my Father, and you are in me, and I am in you" (14:20). Christ would leave the presence of the Spirit with the disciples.

In the second of Jesus' five descriptions of the Advocate, he depicted the Holy Spirit as an interpreter or teacher (14:26). Like us, the apostles didn't always understand what the Savior taught. Like us, the disciples didn't always remember the details of what he said. Jesus explained that the Counselor "will teach you all things and will remind you of everything I have said to you" (14:26). The Spirit does not give new truth, but, as with the disciples, the Spirit enables us to grow in understanding God. The Helper relays messages from the Father and helps us prayerfully comprehend Scripture. Only through the Interpreter and Teacher could John have understood and remembered the words to write the Fourth Gospel.

In Jesus' living will, he bequeathed not only the legacy of the Paraclete but peace also (14:27). The word translated *peace* means a condition of order, harmony, tranquility, and calm. In spite of the dangerous river of events flowing around him, Jesus experienced and offered peace as he led his disciples out of the upper room (14:31).

Counsel (15:26—16:15)

Two days after our camp Guadalupe River flood, the director received a call that a calm, peaceful rise was moving down the river. The program director decided the counselors would take all 306 nervous girls to the waterfront. We sat them on the concrete steps of the amphitheater pier. The campers witnessed the water gently rise and quietly move up a step at a time. The next day, with the water deemed safe, the girls felt comfortable swimming and canoeing on the sparkling Guadalupe.

Only when we have been convicted and have repented and accepted God's grace does the Holy Spirit become our Advocate.

Jesus' internal peace calmed the disciples as they made their way to the Garden of Gethsemane. The Master probably stopped along the way to talk and offer object lessons. At an ancient tree, he discussed abiding in him as a branch remains in the vine in order to bear fruit (15:1–8). The Savior reminded his followers of obedient and sacrificial love, encouraging them to "Love each other as I have loved you" (15:12). He moved them from a master-servant relationship to calling them friends because "everything that I learned from my Father I have made known to you" (15:15). He appointed them to bear his fruit, promised God would answer their prayers, and commanded them to "Love each other" (15:17).

Christ knew that life would be difficult for his followers because the world would hate them (15:18–25). In this context, he gave his third teaching about the Holy Spirit. He explained that the Paraclete would "testify about me" as a witness of grace and truth (15:26). He would illuminate the hearts of those who heard the arguments. Too, in the courtroom of the world, Christ's followers would be empowered by the Spirit as they took the witness stand (15:27).

Jesus warned his followers of persecution (16:1–4). He then provided his fourth teaching about the Holy Spirit. The Counselor could not come "unless I go away" (16:7). Then the Paraclete would become the prosecutor of the world, convicting people of their guilt in sin (16:8–11). The verb translated "convict" carries the meaning of exposing, refuting, convincing, and convicting. Before we accept Christ as Savior, the Holy Spirit "prosecutes" us. Only when we have been convicted and have repented and accepted God's grace does the Holy Spirit become our Advocate.

In his fifth teaching, Jesus showed the Spirit as Revealer. The Paraclete explains the truth so that followers understand the message (16:12–15). The Revealer moves Christians from head-and-heart knowledge to putting hands, feet, and voice to faith. The Holy Spirit would become the disciples' ally in spreading the good news, convicting the world of sin, and leading them to bear fruit and glorify God rather than self.

> *Jesus prayed for our oneness in him just as he prayed that the disciples would be one.*

Jesus honestly discussed the disciples' approaching grief, comparing it to a woman in childbirth who feels pain translated into joy when she holds her baby (16:16–24). Jesus assured them of his love once again, and the disciples finally got it (16:25–30). "You believe at last!" Jesus exclaimed (16:31). He reminded them that he was going away but that he had achieved victory over the world (16:33).

Communication (John 17)

The most difficult aspect of the camp flood I experienced was lack of communication. The phone lines were dead for two days. In a time before cell phones, frustrated and frantic parents longed to converse with their daughters. When the sun came out, one dad rented a plane. He buzzed the camp as the girls communicated with waves and cheers. My boyfriend at

The Holy Spirit at Work Through the Gospel of John

In Isaiah 55:11, God promised that his word would not return to him empty. Relying on that promise and the Holy Spirit, Pastor Israel Rodriquez and Primera Iglesia Bautista members in Piedras Negras on the Texas-Mexico border saturated their city with God's word. Texas Baptists assisted by providing 42,000 Gospels of John. The church saw people come to Christ every week. A similar project in Juarez across the Rio Grande from El Paso has yielded the same kind of results.

What can your church and the Holy Spirit do in your community?

the time later admitted that even though I was a counselor, he wanted to hear my voice, too.

While Jesus remained with them, the disciples enjoyed daily communication with him. He had already taught them the Lord's Prayer (Matthew 6:9–13), but in his final conversation with God before the crucifixion, Jesus offered a last lesson in prayer and consistent communication with the Father. He demonstrated both the form and the content of conversation with God.

Perhaps Christ stopped at a spot just outside the temple area as he moved toward the garden. First, he briefly prayed for himself, addressing God as Holy Father and expressing awe and intimacy (John 17:1). Then he prayed that he would glorify God in completing his assigned work on earth (17:2–5).

In the longest part of the prayer, Jesus interceded for his earthly disciples as a group (17:6–19). He thanked God for them and asked that God protect them so they might be one (17:11). As they listened to his prayer, the disciples were once again assured that Jesus would not leave them orphaned (17:11; see 14:18). The Master gave them to God's safekeeping (17:12–15). Finally, he set them apart for his joyful service, "As you sent me into the world, I have sent them into the world" (17:18).

If we choose Jesus, we will never be alone.

Last, the Savior prayed for future believers (17:20–26). That includes you and me! Jesus prayed for our oneness in him just as he prayed that the disciples would be one. He requested that same spiritual unity so that the world might believe (17:21). He closed by asking that we be with him in glory and that "the love you have for me may be in them and that I myself may be in them" (17:26).

With his prayer finished, Jesus could safely leave his disciples in the hands of the Holy Spirit as he faced the crisis of the cross.

Change

When our children were young, they loved hearing the story of how their mother survived the flood when she was a camp counselor. My husband John joked that it had grown as big as Noah's experience in the ark! Then our sons went to a boys' camp on the Guadalupe. As we drove from Kerrville to Hunt, I showed Marshall, Michael, and Holly where the power of the rushing water changed the course of the river. Houses that had been waterfront property were yards away while others were closer than planned. The landscape changed forever.

Jesus' death changed the landscape of the disciples' world forever, but he prepared them to live on a changing earth. Today, we live in a change-driven world. When Jesus left the earth, he did not leave his disciples or Christians of any generation orphaned. He sent the Holy Spirit as Comforter, Teacher, Witness, Prosecutor, and Revealer.

Jesus never promised we would lead problem-free lives. Instead, if we love and obey him, Jesus promises his presence, his protection, and his peace. He offers loving and supportive relationships within the community of Christians. He prays for each of us and promises to return again.

Jesus set before us two ways to live: without him or with him. Judas chose without him. The other eleven chose him and were never alone. If we choose Jesus, we will never be alone. He sends the Paraclete to dwell within us and walk alongside us. He provides comfort, counsel, and completion of the Father's work in our lives. He offers the privilege of communication with God in prayer. Have you made your choice? Does the Holy Spirit live inside your heart and soul?

QUESTIONS

1. What sources of encouragement and strength did Jesus leave for the disciples?

2. Are these the same for us today? Why or why not?

3. How does the Paraclete or Holy Spirit minister to us?

4. What are some ways the world knows that we are Christians and that the Holy Spirit lives in us?

5. How does the Spirit help us face the challenges of a changing world?

Focal Text

John 19:1–21, 26–30

Background

John 18—19

Main Idea

Jesus willingly gave his life to fulfill his mission of drawing all people to himself.

Question to Explore

What was "finished" at Jesus' crucifixion?

Study Aim

To explain how Jesus' death affects my life today

Study and Action Emphases

- Affirm the Bible as our authoritative guide for life and ministry
- Share the gospel with all people
- Develop a growing, vibrant faith

LESSON TWELVE

"It Is Finished"

Quick Read

The Gospel of John portrays the events prior to the crucifixion and describes Jesus' death on the cross as Jesus willingly lay down his life to provide salvation to all people of all times.

My father served as county attorney in Eldorado, Texas, during my grow-
ing-up years. When I reached fourth grade, the school bell dismissed my
younger sister and me an hour apart. So Mother wouldn't have to drive
back into town, I walked to the courthouse and "worked" for Daddy every
afternoon, answering the phone and filing. The sheriff, judge, highway
patrolman, and other officials became my friends.

Then I reached driving age. I shook as I drove with the highway patrolman in the passenger seat. I knew Daddy and his friends were watching
from the courthouse windows. Once I earned my driver's license, I lived in
fear of speeding. I just knew the sheriff would arrest me, I would appear
before the judge, my dad would help them throw the book at me, and
everyone else would mercilessly tease me. It seems silly now, but butterflies
flew inside when I got behind the wheel. I never did get a ticket, but I
drove with that troubled spirit until I left for college.

Jesus never did anything wrong. Yet he faced arrest and the cruelest of
punishments.

Untroubled Spirit: The Betrayal (18:1–11)

The Gospel of John records that after Jesus' prayer for the disciples in John
17, he led them (minus Judas) across the Kidron, or brook of cedars, to an
olive grove (John 18:1). Anticipating finding Jesus there in the dark night,
Judas met them with armed Roman soldiers and Jewish temple police
(18:2–3). Jesus asked whom they wanted. When the answer, "Jesus of
Nazareth," came, he identified himself (18:4–5).

Amazingly, awe arrested the arresters. "They drew back and fell to the
ground" (18:6). Jesus remained calm as he allowed his arrest but asked that
his followers be released. Simon Peter drew his sword, cutting off the high
priest's servant's ear. Jesus chastised him, saying (18:11), "Put your sword
away! Shall I not drink the cup the Father has given me?"

Unshakeable Resolve: The Arrest and Jewish Trial (18:12–27)

The detachment of Roman soldiers and Jewish officials didn't need their
weapons when they arrested Jesus. They didn't need to bind him although
they did (18:12). Jesus' unshakeable resolve to fulfill his mission of drawing all people to his salvation allowed him to be arrested willingly.

John 19:1–21, 26–30

¹Then Pilate took Jesus and had him flogged. ²The soldiers twisted together a crown of thorns and put it on his head. They clothed him in a purple robe ³and went up to him again and again, saying, "Hail, king of the Jews!" And they struck him in the face.

⁴Once more Pilate came out and said to the Jews, "Look, I am bringing him out to you to let you know that I find no basis for a charge against him." ⁵When Jesus came out wearing the crown of thorns and the purple robe, Pilate said to them, "Here is the man!"

⁶As soon as the chief priests and their officials saw him, they shouted, "Crucify! Crucify!"

But Pilate answered, "You take him and crucify him. As for me, I find no basis for a charge against him."

⁷The Jews insisted, "We have a law, and according to that law he must die, because he claimed to be the Son of God."

⁸When Pilate heard this, he was even more afraid, ⁹and he went back inside the palace. "Where do you come from?" he asked Jesus, but Jesus gave him no answer. ¹⁰"Do you refuse to speak to me?" Pilate said. "Don't you realize I have power either to free you or to crucify you?"

¹¹Jesus answered, "You would have no power over me if it were not given to you from above. Therefore the one who handed me over to you is guilty of a greater sin."

¹²From then on, Pilate tried to set Jesus free, but the Jews kept shouting, "If you let this man go, you are no friend of Caesar. Anyone who claims to be a king opposes Caesar."

¹³When Pilate heard this, he brought Jesus out and sat down on the judge's seat at a place known as the Stone Pavement (which in Aramaic is Gabbatha). ¹⁴It was the day of Preparation of Passover Week, about the sixth hour.

"Here is your king," Pilate said to the Jews.

¹⁵But they shouted, "Take him away! Take him away! Crucify him!"

"Shall I crucify your king?" Pilate asked.

"We have no king but Caesar," the chief priests answered.

¹⁶Finally Pilate handed him over to them to be crucified.

So the soldiers took charge of Jesus. ¹⁷Carrying his own cross, he went out to the place of the Skull (which in Aramaic is called Golgotha). ¹⁸Here they crucified him, and with him two others—one on each side and Jesus in the middle.

¹⁹Pilate had a notice prepared and fastened to the cross. It read: JESUS OF NAZARETH, THE KING OF THE JEWS. ²⁰Many of the Jews read this sign, for the place where Jesus was crucified was near the city, and the

sign was written in Aramaic, Latin and Greek. [21]The chief priests of the Jews protested to Pilate, "Do not write 'The King of the Jews,' but that this man claimed to be king of the Jews."

. . . .

[26]When Jesus saw his mother there, and the disciple whom he loved standing nearby, he said to his mother, "Dear woman, here is your son," [27]and to the disciple, "Here is your mother." From that time on, this disciple took her into his home.

[28]Later, knowing that all was now completed, and so that the Scripture would be fulfilled, Jesus said, "I am thirsty." [29]A jar of wine vinegar was there, so they soaked a sponge in it, put the sponge on a stalk of the hyssop plant, and lifted it to Jesus' lips. [30]When he had received the drink, Jesus said, "It is finished." With that, he bowed his head and gave up his spirit.

Jesus faced a speedy trial in two phases: a Jewish trial and a Roman trial. The soldiers first took the Savior to Annas, former high priest who was father-in-law of the current high priest Caiaphas (18:13). Annas was no longer high priest, but he remained the power in the background.

At least two disciples, Simon Peter and another, followed Jesus (18:15). In the high priest's courtyard, Peter denied Christ for the first time. With the other apostle inside, Annas "questioned Jesus about his disciples and his teaching" (18:19). Perhaps Jesus was accused of being a false prophet who secretly led others away from God and thus should be put to death (Deuteronomy 13:1–10). Jesus answered that he openly taught in the temple and in synagogues (John 18:20).

After one of the officials slapped the Lord, Annas sent the restrained prisoner to Caiaphas (18:22–24). The Gospel of John describes how afterward they took him to Pontius Pilate, the Roman governor (18:28). As the Jewish leaders questioned Jesus and then led him away, Peter denied the Master for the second and third times just before the cock crowed (18:25–27).

Unworthy Sentence: The Roman Trial and Sentence (18:28—19:16)

When a trial was held in my hometown courthouse, Daddy frequently let me watch from the back. I don't remember many specifics of these trials, but I do remember the specifics of a trial produced at an evening worship time at camp. In "The Trial of Pontius Pilate," the judge chose jurors by drawing names from the audience. I wasn't chosen, but my best friend was. The prosecutor charged Pilate with the death of Jesus of Nazareth. The defense attorney argued that the Jewish religious leaders, the Jewish people, and all those for whom Christ died jointly bore the blame. Pilate simply found himself in a precarious position. To protect his job, he acquiesced to those who sought Jesus' death. These twenty-five years later, I remember the arguments, but I don't remember the verdict. It didn't seem to matter because there was enough guilt for everyone.

Jesus willingly gave up his own life.

Pontius Pilate served as Roman governor of Judea. After the death of Herod and his son Archelaus, Rome put Judea under control of a procurator or governor. Pilate became governor in AD 26 and maintained both financial and judicial control over the area.

Pilate served at the pleasure of the Roman emperor. The Jews hated Pilate because he hung worship images of the emperor and minted coins containing pagan religious symbols. Some say Pilate took money from the sacred treasure of the temple to build an aqueduct for the city. Rumor had it he took bribes. Historians of the time depict Pilate as an authoritarian but practical ruler. His primary goal was to keep the peace and therefore keep his job.

I just knew the sheriff would arrest me, I would appear before the judge, my dad would help them throw the book at me, and everyone else would mercilessly tease me.

Pilate usually lived in Caesarea on the coast but traveled to Jerusalem for official duties. During feast days such as Passover, Pilate arrived with extra troops to maintain control of zealots. Although his official residence in the city was the palace, Pilate sometimes stayed at the secure fortress that overlooked the temple.

The Jewish leaders took Jesus to Pilate early in the morning, probably before 6 a.m. They refused to enter the palace or fortress because entering a Gentile residence would have made them unclean for the Passover (18:28). Ironically, they kept the ceremonial law so they could eat the Passover lamb while seeking to kill the Lamb of God. The governor went outside to talk with them. He tried to send Jesus away with them, but the Jewish leaders wanted Jesus crucified, a sentence they could not impose (18:29–32).

Pilate finally took Jesus inside and asked (18:33), "Are you the king of the Jews?" After his conversation with Jesus, Pilate found that the Lord hadn't committed a crime that would stand in Roman court (18:34–38). However, he gave the Jews an opportunity to release Jesus through the traditional Passover pardon of one criminal. They chose instead the notorious Barabbas (18:39–40).

Pilate knew the truth but lacked the courage to release the Savior. He had not found Jesus guilty of a crime but still had Jesus illegally beaten on his back with a rod or whip, a flogging that severely weakened and frequently killed prisoners (19:1). The soldiers crowned Christ with thorns, robed him in royal purple, and mocked him with Pilate's words, "Hail, king of the Jews!" (19:3; see 18:33–39).

Pilate tried once again to release Jesus. He paraded the beaten Lamb of God before them, explaining, "I find no basis for a charge against him" (19:4–5). The chief priests and other religious leaders still demanded crucifixion, claiming Jesus should die because he said he was "the Son of God" (19:6–7).

The frightened governor took Jesus inside for more questioning. Pilate needed to know whether Jesus came from earth or heaven (19:8–9). Christ's silence bothered Pilate (19:10). The Savior knew that while Pilate had earthly authority over him, real authority came from his Father in heaven. Too, the Jewish leaders had committed the "greater sin" (19:11).

Pilate knew the truth but lacked the courage to release the Savior.

Pilate tried once more to release Jesus, but the Jews dealt the final blow with their threat of another negative report to the emperor, "Anyone who claims to be a king opposes Caesar" (19:12). The governor felt helpless against their blackmail. Thus, about 6 a.m. on the day before Passover itself, he sentenced Jesus of Nazareth to crucifixion and turned him over to the soldiers (19:13–16). Jesus came to his own Jewish people, but they did not receive him. Instead, their leaders secured his death (1:11).

Undeniable Love: The Crucifixion (19:17–30)

Three times during the last eight years, my husband John and I relearned the topics of the Amendments to the Constitution of the United States of America as each of our children memorized them for high school government. Amendment VIII concerns "Cruel and Unusual Punishment" and states, "Excessive bail shall not be required, nor excessive fines imposed, nor cruel and unusual punishments inflicted." Crucifixion qualifies as cruel punishment, the cruelest form of execution imaginable.

According to Roman custom, Jesus carried his own cross to a public area near the city wall called "the place of the Skull" or "Golgotha" (19:17). Generally, the condemned bore only the crossbeam on a parade through the city because the upright shaft was already affixed in the ground.

Pilate chose the notice, "JESUS OF NAZARETH, THE KING OF THE JEWS," written in Aramaic, Latin, and Greek (19:19–20).

Customarily, an inscription containing the name and crime of the accused hung at the top of the shaft. Pilate chose the notice, "JESUS OF NAZARETH, THE KING OF THE JEWS," written in Aramaic, Latin, and Greek (19:19–20). The Jewish religious leaders demanded that Pilate change the words to show that Jesus only claimed to be the king of the Jews. Pilate finally chose to exert his authority and power. He refused (19:21–22).

In crucifixion, executioners fastened the victim's outstretched arms to the crossbeam and then affixed the crossbeam to the upright shaft. Finally, the feet were nailed or bound to the shaft. In Roman executions, the victim's clothing belonged to the executioners. Before the soldiers placed Jesus on the cross, they stripped him of his garments, probably consisting of a robe, tunic or undergarment, belt, sandals, and head covering (19:23). Each of the four executioners took a piece of clothing. The undergarment, though, was seamless, and so they cast lots for it (19:24; Psalm 22:18).

Ironically, they kept the ceremonial law so they could eat the Passover lamb while seeking to kill the Lamb of God.

As Jesus hung on the cross, he saw his mother standing near "the disciple whom he loved" (19:26). In spite of his agony, he spoke lovingly to Mary as he placed his mother in the disciple's care (19:25–27). "Later," says the Gospel of John, knowing he had completed the work he came from heaven to do, Jesus said, "I am thirsty" (19:28). The Romans soaked a sponge in vinegar and lifted it up to Jesus (19:29; see Psalm 69:21).

Then Jesus uttered his last words, "It is finished," and "gave up his spirit" (John 19:30). The words carry the meaning of finishing a task or a responsibility. The Messiah was saying, *It is accomplished.*

Jesus willingly gave up his own life. No one took it from him. No person or government had that power (10:18). His death on the cross confirmed his words, "But I, when I am lifted up from the earth, will draw all men to myself" (12:32). Jesus died so he could draw you and me and all people of all times to his salvation.

Unspeakable Grief: The Burial (19:31–42)

During the centennial of Woman's Missionary Union in 1988, WMU marked the graves of its presidents, executive directors, and founders from the states. WMU placed a plaque on the grave of Texan Marie Mathis, president from 1956–1963 and 1969–1975. Waco women felt disappointed that the marker for the woman who had served while living in Waco had to be in Dalhart.

Jesus died so he could draw you and me and all people of all times to his salvation.

Then through circumstances only God could direct, we discovered the grave of the WMU founder from Arkansas in Waco's Oakwood Cemetery. Margretta Adelaide "Dettie" Dudgeon Goolsby Early and her husband lived briefly in Waco where he hurriedly buried her on the day she died, June 20, 1894.

Restorative Justice

In 1986, Texas Baptist Men built Hospitality House in Huntsville, Texas, as a place for family members to stay while seeing prisoners at the penitentiary there. Since 1987, Nelda and Bob Norris have hosted parents, siblings, wives, and children, providing clean beds, hearty meals, and God's grace.

They have loved nearly 150 families through executions of family members. When Nelda speaks in churches, she explains those nights. Mothers usually hurt most because they remember the tiny baby's smile, the first day of school, the holidays, and the hugs. Chaplain Jim Brazzil joins the Norrises and the family after the execution. He spends the final day with each offender, offering Christ's love and a listening heart. Another chaplain stays with the victim's family members.

But inmates, victims, and their families aren't the only people who need the touch of Jesus. Consider criminal justice system employees, judges, attorneys, former inmates, and even those who must clean up crime scenes. Those involved in this ministry minister to all these, letting them know that they are not by themselves and that God's love makes a difference.

Her grave was marked with a short inscription on a tiny stone, "Dettie, wife of M. D. Early." We obtained a centennial marker from WMU, engraved it with her full name and WMU significance, and laid it on her grave in a memorial service.

Jesus had no memorial service or grave prepared. Bodies of the executed belonged to Rome, and crucifixion sometimes took hours or days to inflict death unless the executioners broke the legs of the condemned. Because of the approaching Sabbath, Jewish leaders requested that Pilate have the three crucified men's legs broken and the bodies removed from the crosses. The soldiers broke the legs of the two others. Knowing the Savior was dead, the soldiers instead stuck a spear in his side, "bringing a sudden flow of blood and water" (19:34; see Psalm 34:20).

Jesus had fulfilled his Father's mission. It was finished.

Often the bodies of those crucified were thrown away or left for vultures. But Joseph of Arimathea, a member of the Sanhedrin, asked Pilate for permission to take Jesus' body (John 19:38; Mark 15:43). Nicodemus who "visited Jesus at night" brought spices (John 19:39). The two secret disciples showed their faith by providing Jesus with a beautiful burial in a new garden tomb (19:40–42).

Jesus had fulfilled his Father's mission. It was finished.

QUESTIONS

1. Who was really responsible for Jesus death? Why?

2. What would you have done if you had held Pilate's position as governor?

3. How do you think Jesus' trial and execution affected the Jewish religious leaders?

4. Why did Jesus give up his spirit with the words, "It is finished" (19:30)?

5. What does Jesus' death mean to you today?

Focal Text

John 20:1–2, 11–29

Background

John 20—21

Main Idea

Jesus' resurrection appearances confirm his identity as God's Son and commission us to be his messengers to the world.

Question to Explore

What does Jesus have yet to do for you to believe in him, serve him, and bear witness of him?

Study Aim

To confess my faith in Jesus as Lord

Study and Action Emphases

- Affirm the Bible as our authoritative guide for life and ministry
- Share the gospel with all people
- Develop a growing, vibrant faith
- Include all God's family in decision-making and service
- Value all people as created in the image of God
- Obey and serve Jesus by meeting physical, spiritual, and emotional needs
- Equip people for servant leadership

LESSON THIRTEEN

Seeing and Believing

Quick Read

God confirms Jesus' identity through the empty tomb, the resurrection appearances, and changed lives. As Jesus prepared to return to heaven, he commissioned all believers, including us, to be witnesses for him on earth.

When I was a senior in high school, Mr. Whitaker entered me in the district writing contest. Contestants had two hours to write an essay of no maximum or minimum length on one of two topics. Neither topic excited me at the time, but as soon as I submitted my theme, I knew I had chosen the wrong subject. I don't remember now the topic I chose, but I should have chosen, "Discuss the truth of the adage, 'It's always darkest before the dawn.'" At the moment my fingers released the paper, Good Friday and Easter Sunday immediately flashed through my mind.

Proof of the Resurrection: The Empty Tomb (20:1–9)

The disciples and Jesus' other followers experienced the blackest darkness of their lives when Jesus died on the cross. They watched their hopes and dreams crucified with their Lord. Before sunrise on Sunday morning, Mary Magdalene made her way to the garden where Joseph of Arimathea and Nicodemus had buried Jesus. She wanted to be there at first light. As the morning dawned, she couldn't believe her eyes. Someone had removed the stone from the tomb's entrance and taken the body (20:1). Who could have done this? Jewish leaders surely made the suspect list.

This was no little rock. Typically, to cover a grave, a massive stone, six to seven feet in diameter, was placed in a groove and rolled on a downhill slope until it rested on another large rock or the side of a hill. Moving the heavy, cumbersome stone to reveal the opening required several strong people to shove it back uphill and secure it in place.

As Mary Magdalene ran to tell the news, she reached Simon Peter and "the other disciple, the one Jesus loved" (20:2). She breathlessly told them, "They have taken the Lord out of the tomb, and we don't know where they have put him!"

"The other disciple outran Peter and reached the tomb first" (20:4). This disciple didn't go inside but instead peeked in to see "strips of linen lying there" (20:5). Peter didn't hesitate to enter the grave, however. Peter barreled in, noting not only the linen but also the neatly folded head cloth (20:6–7). The scene would have appeared far too orderly for robbers. They would have left a messy pile of grave clothes. "The other disciple" finally entered the tomb. Although he didn't yet fully understand everything, "He saw and believed" (20:8).

John 20:1–2, 11–29

¹Early on the first day of the week, while it was still dark, Mary Magdalene went to the tomb and saw that the stone had been removed from the entrance. ²So she came running to Simon Peter and the other disciple, the one Jesus loved, and said, "They have taken the Lord out of the tomb, and we don't know where they have put him!"

• •

¹¹ . . . Mary stood outside the tomb crying. As she wept, she bent over to look into the tomb ¹²and saw two angels in white, seated where Jesus' body had been, one at the head and the other at the foot.

¹³They asked her, "Woman, why are you crying?"

"They have taken my Lord away," she said, "and I don't know where they have put him." ¹⁴At this, she turned around and saw Jesus standing there, but she did not realize that it was Jesus.

¹⁵"Woman," he said, "why are you crying? Who is it you are looking for?"

Thinking he was the gardener, she said, "Sir, if you have carried him away, tell me where you have put him, and I will get him."

¹⁶Jesus said to her, "Mary."

She turned toward him and cried out in Aramaic, "Rabboni!" (which means Teacher).

¹⁷Jesus said, "Do not hold on to me, for I have not yet returned to the Father. Go instead to my brothers and tell them, 'I am returning to my Father and your Father, to my God and your God.'"

¹⁸Mary Magdalene went to the disciples with the news: "I have seen the Lord!" And she told them that he had said these things to her.

¹⁹On the evening of that first day of the week, when the disciples were together, with the doors locked for fear of the Jews, Jesus came and stood among them and said, "Peace be with you!" ²⁰After he said this, he showed them his hands and side. The disciples were overjoyed when they saw the Lord.

²¹Again Jesus said, "Peace be with you! As the Father has sent me, I am sending you." ²²And with that he breathed on them and said, "Receive the Holy Spirit. ²³If you forgive anyone his sins, they are forgiven; if you do not forgive them, they are not forgiven."

²⁴Now Thomas (called Didymus), one of the Twelve, was not with the disciples when Jesus came. ²⁵So the other disciples told him, "We have seen the Lord!"

But he said to them, "Unless I see the nail marks in his hands and put my finger where the nails were, and put my hand into his side, I will not believe it."

[26]A week later his disciples were in the house again, and Thomas was with them. Though the doors were locked, Jesus came and stood among them and said, "Peace be with you!" [27]Then he said to Thomas, "Put your finger here; see my hands. Reach out your hand and put it into my side. Stop doubting and believe."

[28]Thomas said to him, "My Lord and my God!"

[29]Then Jesus told him, "Because you have seen me, you have believed; blessed are those who have not seen and yet have believed."

Proof of the Resurrection:
The Appearance to Mary Magdalene (20:10–17)

Our daughter Holly called from Howard Payne University with a question. A New Testament test loomed the next day. Dr. Grambling's review included the question, "List the resurrection appearances of Jesus." Her notes seemed somewhat confused. Which Bible book contained the list? We discussed how the gospel writers highlighted different aspects of the Easter story, and even when several people witness the same event, they take away varying impressions. Matthew, Mark, Luke, and John don't each include all of Jesus' appearances. The Gospel of John describes four of them.

The disciples and Jesus' other followers experienced the blackest darkness of their lives when Jesus died on the cross.

The disciples left for their homes, but Mary lingered in the garden, grieving for her Master (20:10–11). She likely sobbed uncontrollably. The Jewish leaders and Roman government had executed the person who believed in her and loved her. Now, they had stolen his body. As she looked in the tomb, she glimpsed heaven's power in two angels seated where Jesus' head and feet had been (20:12).

"Woman, why are you crying?" they asked (20:13). As Mary Magdalene explained her loss, she turned and saw Jesus through her tears. She mistook him for the gardener and responded to his question about her weeping with a request. "Sir . . . tell me where you have put him, and I will get him" (20:15).

Then Jesus spoke her name with tenderness and love. Perhaps Mary knelt down and clasped his feet as she cried joyous tears, exclaiming "Rabboni!" This Aramaic word means *teacher* (20:16). In the next moments, her Lord told her to stop clinging to him. Just as we want to hold on to a loved one we haven't seen in a long time or don't expect to see again, Mary wanted to be near her Savior. Instead, Jesus commissioned her as the first missionary to tell others that he lived (20:17).

The resurrection confirms Jesus' identity as God's Son, the Messiah, who sacrificed himself to overcome sin and death for all humankind. The word for resurrection simply means *to stand up again*. Jesus *stood up again* to save us.

Proof of the Resurrection:
The Appearance to the Ten Disciples (20:18–23)

My grandmother saw significant changes during her lifetime—the first automobile, the first airplane, the first motion pictures, the first television, the first man into space, and the first computer. She felt the greatest change came in the status of women, however. She was old enough to vote when the Nineteenth Amendment gave women that right in 1920. She witnessed the 1925 inauguration of Texas' Miriam A. Ferguson, the second female governor (by two weeks) in the United States. (The first state to have a female governor was Wyoming.)[1] She rejoiced with the election of the first women to the United States House and Senate. Ma taught school for forty-eight years, treating girls and boys equally. She encouraged me to follow my dreams with the words, "You can do anything you set your mind to." After all, my grandfather would say, "Jesus first appeared to Mary Magdalene on Easter."

> *The resurrection confirms Jesus' identity as God's Son, the Messiah, who sacrificed himself to overcome sin and death for all humankind.*

Imagine the disciples' astonishment when Mary Magdalene rushed to share the joyful news. Heavenly sunlight flooded her earthly darkness. Not only had Christ risen from the dead, but also he had appeared first to her, a woman (20:18).

Society viewed women as second-class citizens. In fact, Roman law considered women the same as children. They couldn't testify in court. Only with the approval of the nearest male relative or a guardian could a

Eloise Glass Cauthen: Never Too Young and Never Too Old To Be Sent

Eloise Glass was born in China to missionaries. As a girl, she heard God's call to missions herself and attended Baylor University and Southwestern Seminary to prepare. The missions volunteer fell in love with Baylor friend Baker James Cauthen from Lufkin, Texas. Baker felt called to serve as a pastor, not as a missionary. After their marriage, however, God called Baker James Cauthen, too.

The Cauthens sailed to China in 1939. They were assigned to Chefoo (Yantai) where Eloise had grown up. In 1941, the advancing Japanese army forced the family to flee, leaving Eloise's beloved piano. They returned in 1946 but fled again in 1948. After serving in Hong Kong, Baker James Cauthen became Executive Secretary of the Foreign Mission Board in Richmond, Virginia. From 1953–1979, Baptists called Eloise the "first lady of foreign missions."

Eloise never dreamed she would see China again. But the country opened to teachers. Widowed in 1985, Eloise accepted an invitation to teach English at Yantai University. She was seventy-six years old. She found the nearby church building where she and her husband had served. As she entered, her eyes fell on the piano, the one left behind forty-five years earlier. The Chinese Christians assured her how important the instrument had been.

Eloise died in 1995, knowing that she had never been too young or too old to be sent by God.

---

female execute a will, sign a contract, sell property, or accept an inheritance. Many believed women to be intellectually inferior, a source of temptation, and necessary only to bear children and oversee a household.

> After all, my grandfather would say, "Jesus first appeared to Mary Magdalene on Easter."

Jesus' actions toward women showed respect, love, and boldness (4:6–26; 8:3–11). Jesus significantly raised the status of women.

Perhaps the apostles questioned Mary's words. We don't know. We do know the ten disciples didn't show confidence in a risen Savior. They were frightened and without Thomas when they locked themselves in a room to share their broken dreams and broken cause (20:24). Jesus' enemies had crucified him. Would they kill his followers, too?

Suddenly, Jesus appeared as he had earlier promised (20:19; see 14:18–19). Just as Jesus had done in the upper room the evening before his crucifixion, he offered his peace, a greeting filled with order, harmony, tranquility, calm, and comfort (20:19; see 14:27). Surely the disciples' mouths flew open in amazement. They recognized their Lord. Closed doors couldn't keep their Savior out. Then he showed them his sword-pierced side and the nail holes in his wrists. Seeing was believing as the atmosphere shifted from excruciating fear to exhilarating joy just as he said it would (20:20; see 16:22).

Everyone surely talked at once, greeting their Master and expressing their excitement. Jesus calmed them by repeating (20:21), "Peace be with you!" His commission of the disciples echoed his prayer for them in the garden (see 17:18). "As the Father has sent me, I am sending you" (20:21). Then the Savior breathed into them the promise of a Spirit-filled, Spirit-

Jesus significantly raised the status of women.

guided witness through the *Paraclete*, just as he had pledged in his farewell teachings (20:22; see 16:7). They should proclaim God's love, grace, glory, and forgiveness (20:23). Christ encouraged, equipped, enabled, and empowered them and consequently us today to spread the good news of his salvation.

Proof of the Resurrection: The Appearance to Thomas and the Other Disciples (20:24–31)

Surely the disciple Thomas wouldn't be proud of the nickname given him by generations of Christians. The Bible identifies Thomas also as Didymus, but we call him "Doubting" Thomas. The Gospel of John doesn't explain why Thomas wasn't with the other apostles on Easter night. John does say that the others told Thomas they had seen the risen Lord. But for Thomas, hearing wasn't believing. Seeing was. "Unless I see the nail marks in his hands . . . I will not believe it" (20:25). Perhaps we shouldn't be too hard on Thomas. After all, Jesus had shown the others his hands and his side without their asking (20:20).

The Sunday after Easter the disciples met again, but this time Thomas came. Once again Jesus appeared in spite of locked doors. Once again Jesus offered the comfort of his greeting (20:26), "Peace be with you!" The Master Teacher looked straight at Thomas and invited him to touch and see his hands and feel his side. Then Jesus spoke the words that led to the disciple's nickname, "Stop doubting and believe" (20:27). The Gospel of John doesn't indicate that Thomas touched the Savior before gloriously

145

and powerfully confessing Jesus as "My Lord and my God!" (20:28). What a powerful confession of faith by Thomas!

As Jesus affirmed Thomas, he offered a beatitude or blessing for all "who have not seen and yet have believed" (20:29). That includes you and me and every Christian of every generation who did not see Christ physically. Thomas and the others believed because they saw and experienced the Savior. We believe, not because we see with our eyes, but because we see with our hearts through the Holy Spirit.

John couldn't include in his gospel all that he saw and experienced during his time with Jesus. The apostle, though, chose specific words and stories so that we might believe in Christ, the Son of God, and have eternal life through him (20:30–31).

Proof of the Resurrection: The Testimony of Changed Lives (21:1–25)

The first Sunday in June, many Texas Baptists gather at the old church in Independence for worship, dinner on the grounds, and the presentation of the Texas Baptist Elder Statesman Award. That weekend becomes a homecoming as we return to our roots.

In changing times, we seek familiar routines and recognizable faces. We long to feel the warmth of grandmother's quilt, to taste homemade peach cobbler, to hear stories at a family reunion, to watch a game at the old high school field. In short, we long for the comfort of home.

The disciples were no different in their day. When Jesus left them, Peter, Thomas, Nathanael, James, John, and two other disciples returned home to the Sea of Galilee to do what they knew best—fish. They cast their nets all night without catching anything. Then a man they didn't recognize called from the shore for them to move their net to the right side. So many fish filled the seine that the apostles could only drag it (21:1–6). "The disciple whom Jesus loved" recognized Jesus and told Peter (21:7). The impetuous disciple jumped in the water as the others followed in the boat. Christ prepared and served them breakfast of bread and fish on the shore (21:7–14).

Christ encouraged, equipped, enabled, and empowered them and consequently us today to spread the good news of his salvation.

Just as Jesus did in the upper room after supper, the Savior taught his disciples after a meal. He asked Peter this question three times in similar words (21:15; see 21:16–17): "Simon son of John, do you truly love me more than these?" Jesus probably was asking whether Peter still claimed to have greater love for Jesus than the other disciples had. The first two times the Savior used the Greek verb *agapas*, the word meaning *divine love*. This word includes the qualities of loyalty and responsibility. Each time, Peter declared his love with the Greek word meaning *friendship*. The third time, Jesus lowered the level of his question to the Greek verb *phileis*, the love of good friends.

> *We believe, not because we see with our eyes, but because we see with our hearts through the Holy Spirit.*

Some Bible interpreters suggest that Jesus questioned the disciple three times because of Peter's three denials (18:15–18, 25–27). We don't know whether that is true, but we do know that Jesus' words grieved Simon and that the Good Shepherd challenged him to feed his lambs and take care of his sheep (21:15–17). In those moments, Jesus called Simon Peter to assume the role of a shepherd to his flock.

Then Jesus explained that one day Peter would prove his loyalty through his death (21:18–19). Tradition tells us Peter asked to be crucified upside down because he didn't consider himself worthy to die as Christ died. Just like the problem child in a classroom, Peter remained impetuous. "What about him," he wanted to know of "the disciple whom Jesus loved" (21:20–21).

Called and Commissioned

Jesus commissions all of us as missionaries. God still calls people today to full-time ministry. How can we help them respond? Consider how to put these ideas into practice:

- Encourage hands-on missions experiences that develop passion for sharing Christ.
- Establish a climate that values God's vocational call. Eliminate statements such as, "You don't want to be a pastor."
- Never tell children or teens they are too young or adults they are too old.
- Provide a mentor to assist in clarifying, exploring, and preparing for God's call.
- Educate the church about opportunities for mission service.

Jesus' words remind us of a teacher who says to a child, *Don't worry about your neighbor. Worry about yourself. I'll take care of your neighbor.* After this exchange between Simon and Jesus, we never find Simon Peter going back to fishing again. His life changed. He moved from denier to proclaimer of Christ the risen Lord, the one who died that Peter and we might live.

What additional proof do you need in order to believe in Jesus, to serve him, and to bear witness of him?

What proof do we have of the resurrection? An eyewitness to all the events in Jesus' ministry and death wrote down his testimony (21:24–25). The tomb was empty. Jesus appeared to Mary Magdalene, to his disciples, and to others after the resurrection. Too, this Jesus looked alive and well, not like the weak, scourged prisoner who had been crucified. The resurrection made a difference in Peter's life. The resurrection also changed the other apostles as they willingly followed the Savior.

What additional proof do you need in order to believe in Jesus, to serve him, and to bear witness of him? Is the resurrection making a difference in your life?

QUESTIONS

1. What is the evidence that Jesus was really raised from the dead?
2. What is the significance of Jesus' first appearance being to Mary Magdalene?
3. What is the relationship between doubt and faith? What can we discover from Thomas' doubt?
4. How did Jesus' resurrection dramatically change the lives of his disciples and other followers? In what ways has the resurrection changed your life and the lives of those around you?
5. What do Jesus' words, "As the Father has sent me, I am sending you" (20:21), mean to you and other Christians today?

NOTES

1. See the article on Miriam Ferguson in "The Handbook of Texas Online" at www.tsha.utexas.edu/handbook/online.

Our Next New Study

(Available for use beginning June 2003)

Amos, Hosea, Micah

AMOS: A GOD WHO ROARS

Lesson 1	It's for You	Amos 2:4–16
Lesson 2	Judgment on Injustice	Amos 3:9—4:3; 5:10–15; 6:4–7; 8:4–6
Lesson 3	Judgment on Religious Hypocrisy	Amos 4:4–5; 5:18–24
Lesson 4	God's Message Rejected	Amos 7:7–17
Lesson 5	Certain Judgment—and Hope	Amos 9

HOSEA: A GOD WHO JUDGES AND RESTORES

Lesson 6	Trouble in the Family	Hosea 1:1–9
Lesson 7	Restoring the Relationship	Hosea 1:10—2:5, 14–23; 3:1–5
Lesson 8	God's Charges	Hosea 4:1–12; 8:1–10, 14
Lesson 9	God's Yearning Heart	Hosea 11:1–11
Lesson 10	Return to the Lord	Hosea 14

MICAH: WHAT THE LORD REQUIRES

Lesson 11	Where Coveting Leads	Micah 1:1–7; 2:1–9
Lesson 12	When Leaders Sell Out	Micah 3
Lesson 13	Peace Is Coming	Micah 4:1–8; 5:2–5a
Lesson 14	God's Case Against His People	Micah 6:1–8

Additional Resources for Studying Amos, Hosea, and Micah:[1]

Donald E. Gowan. "Amos." Gale A. Yee. "Hosea." Daniel J. Simundson. "Micah." *The New Interpreter's Bible*. Volume VII. Nashville: Abingdon Press, 1996.

James Limburg. *Hosea—Micah*. Interpretation: A Bible Commentary for Teaching and Preaching. Atlanta: John Knox Press, 1988.

Billy K. Smith. *Amos, Obadiah, Jonah*. The New American Commentary. Nashville: Broadman and Holman Publishers, 1995.

Ralph L. Smith. "Amos." Roy L. Honeycutt, Jr. "Hosea." B. Elmo Scoggin. "Micah." *The Broadman Bible Commentary*. Volume 7. Nashville, Tennessee: Broadman Press, 1972.

Ralph L. Smith. *Micah—Malachi*. Word Biblical Commentary. Volume 32. Waco, Texas: Word Books, Publisher, 1984.

Douglas Stuart. *Hosea—Jonah*. Word Biblical Commentary. Volume 31. Waco, Texas: Word Books, Publisher, 1987.

NOTES

1. Listing a book does not imply full agreement by the writers or BAPTISTWAY PRESS® with all of its comments.

How to Order More Bible Study Materials

It's easy! Just fill in the following information. (Note: when the *Teaching Guide* is priced at $2.45, the *Teaching Guide* includes Bible comments for teachers.)
🐾 = Texas specific

Title of item	Price	Quantity	Cost
This Issue:			
Gospel of John—Study Guide	$1.95	_____	_____
Gospel of John—Large Print Study Guide	$1.95	_____	_____
Gospel of John—Teaching Guide	$2.45	_____	_____
Previous Issues Available:			
God's Message in the Old Testament—Study Guide 🐾	$1.95	_____	_____
God's Message in the Old Testament—Teaching Guide 🐾	$1.95	_____	_____
Genesis 12—50: Family Matters—Study Guide	$1.95	_____	_____
Genesis 12—50: Family Matters—Large Print Study Guide	$1.95	_____	_____
Genesis 12—50: Family Matters—Teaching Guide	$2.45	_____	_____
Good News in the New Testament—Study Guide 🐾	$1.95	_____	_____
Good News in the New Testament—Large Print Study Guide 🐾	$1.95	_____	_____
Good News in the New Testament—Teaching Guide 🐾	$2.45	_____	_____
Isaiah and Jeremiah—Study Guide	$1.95	_____	_____
Isaiah and Jeremiah—Large Print Study Guide	$1.95	_____	_____
Isaiah and Jeremiah—Teaching Guide	$2.45	_____	_____
Matthew: Jesus As the Fulfillment of God's Promises— Study Guide 🐾	$1.95	_____	_____
Matthew: Jesus As the Fulfillment of God's Promises— Large Print Study Guide 🐾	$1.95	_____	_____
Matthew: Jesus As the Fulfillment of God's Promises— Teaching Guide 🐾	$2.45	_____	_____
Jesus in the Gospel of Mark—Study Guide	$1.95	_____	_____
Jesus in the Gospel of Mark—Large Print Study Guide	$1.95	_____	_____
Jesus in the Gospel of Mark—Teaching Guide	$2.45	_____	_____
Acts: Sharing God's Good News with Everyone—Study Guide 🐾	$1.95	_____	_____
Acts: Sharing God's Good News with Everyone — Teaching Guide 🐾	$1.95	_____	_____
Romans: Good News for a Troubled World—Study Guide 🐾	$1.95	_____	_____
Romans: Good News for a Troubled World—Teaching Guide 🐾	$1.95	_____	_____
1 Corinthians—Study Guide	$1.95	_____	_____
1 Corinthians—Large Print Study Guide	$1.95	_____	_____
1 Corinthians—Teaching Guide	$2.45	_____	_____
Galatians: By Grace Through Faith, and Ephesians: God's Plan and Our Response—Study Guide 🐾	$1.95	_____	_____
Galatians: By Grace Through Faith, and Ephesians: God's Plan and Our Response—Large Print Study Guide 🐾	$1.95	_____	_____
Galatians: By Grace Through Faith, and Ephesians: God's Plan and Our Response—Teaching Guide 🐾	$2.45	_____	_____
Hebrews and James—Study Guide	$1.95	_____	_____
Hebrews and James—Large Print Study Guide	$1.95	_____	_____
Hebrews and James—Teaching Guide	$2.45	_____	_____
Coming for use beginning June 2003			
Amos, Hosea, Micah—Study Guide	$1.95	_____	_____
Amos, Hosea, Micah—Large Print Study Guide	$1.95	_____	_____
Amos, Hosea, Micah—Teaching Guide	$2.45	_____	_____

Beliefs Important to Baptists

Who in the World Are Baptists, Anyway? (one lesson)	$ .45	_____	_____
Who in the World Are Baptists, Anyway?—Teacher's Edition	$ .55	_____	_____
Beliefs Important to Baptists: I (four lessons)	$1.35	_____	_____
Beliefs Important to Baptists: I—Teacher's Edition	$1.75	_____	_____
Beliefs Important to Baptists: II (four lessons)	$1.35	_____	_____
Beliefs Important to Baptists: II—Teacher's Edition	$1.75	_____	_____
Beliefs Important to Baptists: III (four lessons)	$1.35	_____	_____
Beliefs Important to Baptists: III—Teacher's Edition	$1.75	_____	_____
Beliefs Important to Baptists—Study Guide (one-volume edition; includes all lessons)	$2.35	_____	_____
Beliefs Important to Baptists—Teaching Guide (one-volume edition; includes all lessons)	$1.95	_____	_____

---

*Charges for standard shipping service:

Subtotal up to $20.00	$3.95
Subtotal $20.01—$50.00	$4.95
Subtotal $50.01—$100.00	10% of subtotal
Subtotal $100.01 and up	8% of subtotal

Please allow three weeks for standard delivery. For express shipping service: Call 1–866–249–1799 for information on additional charges.

Subtotal _____

Shipping* _____

TOTAL _____

Number of FREE copies of *Brief Basics for Texas Baptists* needed for leading adult Sunday School department periods _____

Your name   Phone

Your church

Mailing address

City   State   Zip code

MAIL this form with your check for the total amount to
BAPTISTWAY PRESS
Baptist General Convention of Texas
333 North Washington
Dallas, TX 75246-1798
(Make checks to "Baptist Executive Board.")

OR, **FAX** your order anytime to: 214-828-5187, and we will bill you.

OR, **CALL** your order toll-free: 1-866-249-1799 (8:30 a.m.-5:00 p.m., M-F),
and we will bill you.

OR, **E-MAIL** your order to our internet e-mail address: baptistway@bgct.org,
and we will bill you.

We look forward to receiving your order! Thank you!